PRA

OUR SECRET LIFE

★ ★ ★

"There are books that spring merely from the reading of other books. There are also books that recount only second hand experience. Then there are those books in which every word has been hard won, in which the scent of costly battle for excellence rises from every page. Phil Nicaud has given us such a book and we should be grateful."

Stephen Mansfield

New York Times bestselling author, speaker, and coach

"*Our Secret Life* goes right to the core truth about leadership. There is no substitute for a leader's character. The first question we ask about our leaders is, can we trust them? Trust is a leader's currency. We build trust as we reflect a true character that is bigger on the inside than on the outside. We should have only one character, and we all should develop and strengthen our character code."

Dr. Thomas D. Mullins

Founding Pastor, Christ Fellowship Church

"Phil is right. Character is the bedrock foundation of any great leader. Build rock solid character versus sandy character (Matthew 7: 24–27) and your impact will be immense and lasting."

Russ Crosson

Chief Mission Officer, RonaldBlueTrust

"To a Marine, nothing counts more than the character of the men and women who you serve with … not professional knowledge, not mental toughness, not physical toughness. When called upon to grab a helmet and weapon, march to the sound of the guns and the smell of cordite, and fight, it is the Marine's character that will eventually ensure victory. Phil Nicaud's remarkable book not only defines character but serves as a roadmap for each of us to develop and refine *our own* character. If you follow his roadmap, you will discover that your personal and professional life will take a new and exciting turn for the better. You will discover that character truly does count."

Charles C. Krulak

General, U.S. Marine Corps (Ret.)

31st Commandant of the U.S. Marine Corps

"As a hungry student of leadership for the past thirty-plus years, I have seen so much written on the topic. I have known and worked with Phil for the last decade and have been so impressed with his passion, wisdom, and expertise in the area of character-based leadership. Regardless of what and who you lead, *Our Secret Life* will better equip you to focus on what matters most as a leader. Phil has done a wonderful job sharing his wisdom in ways that can help all who spend time in this book."

Daniel Harkavy

Founder and CEO, Building Champions, Inc

"Phil has a dynamic ability to connect with people, help them see their potential, and lead them in a simple and effective plan to fulfill their purpose. *Our Secret Life* helps you understand the importance of living with integrity, and gives you a simple plan to live and lead well. Start reading this book today, and bring others on your journey as you embrace a life of integrity that will lead to a lasting legacy."

Pastor Danny Mequet

Small Groups Pastor, Church of The King

★ ★ ★

OUR SECRET LIFE

★ ★ ★

LEAD AN AUTHENTIC, CONFIDENT, FEARLESS LIFE
BY CREATING YOUR UNIQUE ***CHARACTER CODE***

★ ★ ★

OUR
SECRET
LIFE

★ ★ ★

PHIL NICAUD

ISBN: 978-1-7344222-8-3 (paperback)

Published by Story Chorus

STORY CHORUS

TABLE OF CONTENTS

★ ★ ★

PART TWO:

DESIGN

FOREWORD

★ ★ ★

THIS BOOK CHALLENGED ME from the first time I heard the title. "Our Secret Life" says a lot about the things that generally go unsaid in our lives. First of all, Phil and I have been friends for years, and have encouraged one another in our pursuit of character. We both have been studying, mentoring, and writing about developing character for decades. In this process, we have come to the conclusion that the only way to consistently, sustainably impact this world and create results is living from the inside-out. Phil coaches leaders to set and live up to high standards because he does so himself. *It's all about integrity.*

Phil and I have been grieved as we have watched people live from the outside-in. We have seen brilliant, talented, educated people flame out due to their lack of an inner code and core. Living from the outside-in is an unsustainable way to live. If we constantly respond to what's happening around us, we're living by what Phil calls "default" rather than "design." This is an unhealthy way to live and lead no matter the season of life we are in. Phil clearly illustrates that successful living springs out of our secret, or inside life.

This is my long way to say I love this book! This book is one of the most important resources out there for leaders today.

Besides my admiration for Phil, I'm also excited about this book because of its practicality. I think you will appreciate the way this work is created as a "workshop-in-a-book." It is a resource you can use over and over again. You can even use it to help your loved ones, team members, and co-workers. This content has changed many businesses, organizations, and even families for the better. It can do the same for yours!

I'm so glad you picked up *Our Secret Life*. Read it. Study it. Read it again. Apply the excellent lessons and live well, lead strong, and leave a legacy.

Stephen J. Robinson
Pastor
ChurchoftheKing.com

FULL DISCLOSURE

★ ★ ★

1. **Our Secret Life** ***is primarily written to leaders and influencers regarding character.***

We've designed this book to challenge you to think deeply about the issues facing our society, what leadership role you will play in the future, and how your character will shape our culture and your legacy. Although this book is filled with comical anecdotes and inspirational stories, it is intended to be *informational* and *actionable*. Ultimately, it's our desire that this book will guide you on a journey of self-discovery that can help you maximize your potential.

Just so we're clear, we define a leader as anyone attempting to influence another person. While we share the patterns of high-echelon leaders, the principles and practices will be beneficial to leaders in every walk of life. From parents and teachers, to coaches and CEOs, anyone attempting to influence another human being can greatly benefit from this book.

2. **Our Secret Life** ***challenges you to create your*** **Character Code.**

The work you complete in this book has the power to immediately impact your life and leadership, and because it is documented, it can be passed down to those following after you, thereby impacting your legacy!

In short, through a comprehensive interview and study process of elite leaders, we discovered patterns and paths to consider for leading at the highest levels, without compromising your values. Throughout this journey, we will expose you to our findings, and you will have the opportunity to create your own unique Character Code, giving you a system to achieve the outcomes that you desire. You will also be invited to join a community of like-minded individuals who value growth in every area of their lives and deeply care about making a positive impact.

3. ***Workshop in a book.***

While this "workshop-in-a-book" declares a bold promise, it also carries with it a bold challenge. Like we say at all of our conferences and seminars, "your results are directly dependent upon your efforts."

The way you live your personal and professional life truly matters; everyone is "keying" off of you as a leader.

Whether you've invested in yourself by purchasing this book—or someone invested in you—we want to challenge you to tune in and absorb this material, and to complete the design portion of the book. So many people depend on you to be your best, and we believe that possessing a clear, sterling character gives you a tremendous advantage in stewarding well. The objective is that you take time, develop these plans, and enjoy the fruit of good character that leads to authentic, confident, and fearless leadership.

4. ***Book in three pages.***

I *love* reading CliffsNotes™ and Blinkist™ versions of books, so I can determine for myself if I want to go on the journey of investing my time. Out of respect for busy leaders like you, I decided to give you the entire book in three pages. I am confident that you will not only enjoy the journey and impact, but also recommend or buy this book for a friend, family member, colleague, or group in the future.

5. ***This is a "chapterless" book.***

I wanted to make the book simple but still provide order and structure for reference. ***It is divided into two parts, with ten sections in between.***

Part #1: **Discovery** *(Our research)*
Here, we divulge all of the context, counsel, and conclusions from researching a panel of successful, enduring leaders, including the patterns we discovered.

Part #2: **Design** *(Your work)*
Here, you will design your unique Character Code, *giving you a distinct advantage in your ability to lead and steward at the highest level.*

6. *Taught by you.*

This book is most effective when you teach what you learn to others. It is designed to be practical for you as a leader and for sharing the concepts with those you lead. So I challenge you to put this book to work in your own leadership and give it away to others.

THE BOOK IN THREE PAGES

★ ★ ★

IT'S NEVER BEEN A more exciting time to serve as a leader. Our society stands at the cusp of a "**two-pronged**" crisis with a recent accelerator; the next generation of leaders may be ill-prepared in these challenging days.

The world is poised to be reshaped by the aforementioned crisis. This phenomenon will drive a major shift in the players who will ***lead people*** and ***steward resources*** at the highest levels.

> **Prong One:** The largest ***exodus*** of leadership—by 2030, the seventy-nine million American baby boomers (twenty-six percent of the U.S. population) will have reached the common retirement age of sixty-five.[1]

---

[1]Heimlich, Russell. "Baby Boomers Retire." Pew Research Center, 29 Dec. 2010, www.pewresearch.org/fact-tank/2010/12/29/baby-boomers-retire/.

Prong Two: The largest ***transfer*** of wealth—it has been estimated that a staggering $30 trillion nationally and $68 trillion globally will transfer to the next generation of owners and stewards over the next two decades.[2,3]

Accelerator: The COVID-19 pandemic—this book is being written at the end of March 2020. It is our opinion that the global pandemic, which caused fear, panic, illness, death, and ultimately shut down the world's economy, will serve as an accelerator for the two above-mentioned crises. The U.S. government also passed the largest stimulus bill in the history of the world.[4] We predict that this will reinforce our conclusion.

Our conclusion: **character** and **integrity** will become the chief virtues in the race to seize these leadership and stewardship opportunities. Our research finds that people can generally lead authentic, confident, fearless lives regardless of their moral code. That being said, leaders weak in character and integrity (relative to the highest standards of our society, nation, and organizations we serve) may get passed over. Or worse yet, potentially be selected, and fumble

---

[2]Sigalos, MacKenzie. "$30 Trillion Is about to Change Hands in the US." CNBC, 10 July 2018, www.cnbc.com/2018/06/28/wealth-transfer-baby-boomers-estate-heir-inheri tance.html.

[3]Osterland, Andrew. "What the Coming $68 Trillion Great Wealth Transfer Means for Financial Advisors." CNBC, 21 Oct. 2019, www.cnbc.com/2019/10/21/what-the-68-trillion-great-wealth-transfer-means-for-advisors.html.

[4]Delevingne, Lawrence. "U.S. Stimulus Package Is Biggest Ever, but May Not Be Big Enough." Reuters, Thomson Reuters, 30 Mar. 2020, www.reuters.com/article/us-health-coronavirus-fed-stimulus-analy/u-s-stimulus-package-is-biggest-ever-but-may-not-be-big-enough-idUSKBN21H0E7.

the amazing privilege of carrying the torch of success into the next generation.

Those who take character refinement seriously will have a distinct advantage that distinguishes them above their peers. But leadership roles will not just be handed over. They will have to be earned through a "three-shot" approach of competence, confidence, and character. Competence may get you to the table, but confidence and character will win you the opportunity and sustain you on your leadership journey.

To help you do this, we will:

- Share the societal backdrop of *how* and *why* this phenomenon is occurring
- Detail the opportunity it creates for you as a leader and steward
- Guide you through the process of crafting your unique *Character Code*

We look to history to find the keys to solving present (and future) problems. There is nothing new under the sun. So, I invite you on a journey to better understand how this global transfer of wealth and leadership will affect our world. You will be invited to design your own *Character Code* that will ensure you are part of the next generation of leaders that will rise in an unprecedented way!

PART ONE:

DISCOVERY

SECTION 1:

HOW WE GOT HERE:

GLOBAL CONTEXT

THE *GENESIS* OF THIS "two-pronged" leadership crisis happened nearly seventy-five years ago, as waves of soldiers, nurses, merchant marines, and government contractors returned home from World War II. In the years following, the world experienced the largest number of births in a single generation. From 1944 to 1964, the baby boomer generation was born—over one billion people—with seventy-six million born in the United States alone.[5] In America, this rate outpaced the previous silent generation by more than twenty-five million and the following Generation X by more than twenty million.

[5]Source: U.S. Census Bureau International Programs.

Flag raising on Iwo Jima.

Image courtesy of the United States National Archives.

This incredibly high birth rate was fueled by the joyful return of soldiers coming home to settle down, their lifestyles buoyed by GI bills that promised education, good jobs, and affordable housing.

America loved its soldiers. Patriotism was at an all-time high. World War II, while tragic, unified America. While the soldiers were on the battlefield, many Americans had supported the effort at home by purchasing war bonds, growing their own produce, and rationing supplies. Women had replaced men in community institutions, the workplace, and volunteer positions.

The war effort touched nearly every sector of American society, with almost twelve percent of the population actively serving, and an additional thirty-two percent of Americans working in defense contracts and civil servanthood. Over forty percent of the population

Line of women welders of Shipbuilding Corp., Pascagoula, MS.

Image courtesy of the United States National Archives.

had a direct connection to the war effort. Essentially, everyone knew somebody on the battlefield, and communities enthusiastically embraced soldiers' homecoming.[6]

The end of the war was the start of the American dream for many. That generation, wrapped in its patriotism, unity, and optimism, with all of its spending power and baby-making fervor, has long-since reached retirement age.

---

[6]Eikenberry, Karl W. "Americans and Their Military, Drifting Apart." The New York Times, 27 May 2013, www.nytimes.com/2013/05/27/opinion/americans-and-their-military-drifting-apart.html.

While patriotism is still high today, direct connection to military conflicts and the global war on terrorism is at an all-time low, with less than one percent of Americans on active military duty.[7] This means people have been free to "make babies" at a steadier rate since World War II. Yet today, the American birth rate has plummeted to its lowest number in thirty-two years.[8] As the baby boomers walk out the fourth quarter of their lives, they have unintentionally created the first two crises we mentioned (the Great Transfer of wealth and leadership).

This "silver tsunami," as it has already been named, could lead to major failure if we fumble this generational transition, or it could lead to compounded, sustainable success if we steward it well.[9] Generations X and Y are smaller in size by millions than the boomers, which means the older generation's influence and resources will be distributed among fewer people. The competition will be stronger and the stakes higher than we've ever seen for those positions of leadership and wealth stewardship.

This monumental shift presents an unprecedented opportunity for those who see it for what it truly is. Sterling character and integrity will provide an ideal competitive advantage and a clear distinction for leaders in the years to come. Most importantly, however, it will

---

[7]"Demographics of the U.S. Military." Council on Foreign Relations, Council on Foreign Relations, 2016, www.cfr.org/article/demographics-us-military.

[8]"Vital Statistics Rapid Release." Centers for Disease Control and Prevention, National Center for Health Statistics, May 2019, www.cdc.gov/nchs/data/vsrr/vsrr-007-508.pdf.

[9]Angela R. Payne, 2015. "Intergovernmental Management: The Silver Tsunami Effect, an Essay," Studies in Social Sciences and Humanities, Research Academy of Social Sciences, vol. 2, pages 88–98.

"STERLING CHARACTER AND INTEGRITY WILL PROVIDE AN IDEAL COMPETITIVE ADVANTAGE AND A CLEAR DISTINCTION FOR LEADERS IN THE YEARS TO COME."

infuse our individual leadership with authenticity, confidence, and fearlessness. It will safeguard our personal and professional lives from moral, financial, and ethical failures. And it will help us create enduring legacies for our children and the next generation.

As we will see, all great stewardship starts and ends with great character.

SECTION 2:

WHY IT MATTERS:

PHIL'S CONTEXT

I WAS BORN IN the city of New Orleans in the 1970s. My father was a New Orleans police officer and my mother was a school teacher. As a family of seven, we didn't have many resources growing up, as you can imagine! My parents were both from New Orleans, got married in Chalmette, Louisiana, and settled in East New Orleans when my older brother and I were young. Houses were affordable and the culture was rich. In 1979, we moved to the Northshore of Lake Pontchartrain, where my siblings and I grew up with our fifty-two first cousins! Our family was filled with as much diversity as the city of New Orleans herself. Ancestors from my father's side (the Nicauds) have been traced back to France, Saint-Domingue (modern-day Haiti), Italy, and Lebanon. Ancestors from my mother's side came from Canada (Nova Scotia) and Italy. But make no mistake, both sides of the family were from the "country of New Orleans!"

Me with my father (left) and mother and two siblings (right).

As a young boy growing up on the Northshore, I literally thought I could fly. My siblings and I would watch *Popeye and Pals* and *Superman* on Saturday mornings. We would tuck old pillowcases into our collars, run around the yard, and point our hands out in front of us, making the *SHHRRHHEEE* noise, pretending to fly. After doing this for a long period of time, I started to truly believe I had superhuman powers and would soon lift off, defying the laws of gravity.

One cold winter afternoon, I threw on my '70s corduroy jacket and headed to the iron fence in front of our house. I climbed the brick columns that punctuated the fence. By this time, my father had resigned from the New Orleans Police Department and started a wholesale seafood business. As a result, our driveway was covered in oyster shells. I spent nearly an hour out there by myself. Jump … after jump … after jump … landing on oyster shells, and convinced that on the next jump I would soar into flight.

The brick fence posts 30 years later.

I had moments of doubt, but a pulsing faith kept telling me, “You can do it, son. Keep trying … don’t give up!” This faith has whispered in my ear throughout my life. My older brother, Shane, would always dare me to do things first! Whether I was the first to go down the steep water slide, swoop on the rope swing into the Bogue Falaya River, or leap off of the interstate bridge into the Tchefuncte River, this “faith,” coupled with my brother’s dare, always compelled me to jump first.

I could see that faith at work when I played sports. I could sense it when I joined the Marine Corps as a young man. I could feel it when I finally struck up the nerve to ask the finest woman I had ever

My brothers, sisters, and some cousins.

My wife Alisa and I on our wedding day.

seen for her number at a local bank in Norfolk, Virginia. (That one worked out well for me, by the way! That girl has now been my bride for over twenty-three years, and we have five children together.)

Throughout my life, I've seen this faith grow. When I was a young man, it was an infant faith, believing I could break the laws of gravity. In my thirties, I experienced a faith in God that I had never encountered before. And now, halfway through my forties, I still believe that all things are possible with God and for anyone who believes!

I've discovered that we are not defined by how many crashes we endure on the "oyster shells" of life. We are defined by how we learn from these falls, get back up, and try again with wisdom. We've all scraped our knees, but we're not defined by temporary failures and setbacks. We earn our badges of resilience and success in the midst of these crashes, as we learn to overcome.

My journey in business has been a series of small successes and failures that taught me lessons, strengthened my faith, and prepared me to seize opportunity when it arrives. For instance, my consulting business started in faith. Legendary was born with two anchor clients, both of whom executed contracts within one week of each other. These contracts boasted revenue that would normally take a consultant in my space over a decade to amass. While admittedly this was very attractive, it still took all of the faith I had to risk everything again and start another business. Once more, I found myself leaping off the fence post, but this time, rather than hit the ground, I started to fly. To be quite honest, it scared me a bit. I had no processes. No systems. No brand. I had never made that much income in my life, and I was afraid it wouldn't last.

Here's how it happened …

Prior to starting Legendary, I had a front row seat, witnessing one of the best leaders I've ever served with in action. I was a senior manager in an oil and gas engineering consulting firm. The founder and CEO, Kenny, a mechanical engineer by degree, led the organization according to the values that informed his character. He had a balanced approach of valuing profit, production, and people. His approach was informed by his unique character code, which served him as a guide during times of indecision. It helped him to keep his eye equally on all three of those vital components of running a successful organization.

One Wednesday, he asked me to meet with him in his office. He said to me, "Phil, our friendship is sacred, and your service is invaluable to our organization, but I know that you are entrepreneurial. How about you separate from the company, and I will write a contract for your services on a project basis?"

The next day (Thursday) I received a call from my friend Troy, the founder and CEO of a national organization, inviting me to come have dinner with his partners who were flying in from around the United States. He asked me to speak on the topic of leadership and the power of having a coach in your life. If they liked what I had to say, he promised to sign them all up as my clients. So I had dinner with them, gave the talk the next day, and virtually all of them signed up as clients … and my business, Legendary, was born.

Just like that, I was working with over sixty high-capacity leaders around the United States. I scurried to create my systems and processes, and quickly built trusting relationships with my new clients. They could be honest with me during our sessions because our contract included a strict nondisclosure agreement. Confidentiality was (and still is) *the* foundational value in our company. Because privacy was honored, my clients shared their successes, trials, and even their failures.

As I worked with these great leaders and my relationships with them grew, I saw beyond the public and private dimensions of who they were, into the secret chambers of their lives. Some were perfectly aligned with their moral code (which we discuss in depth in the sections ahead). Others were misaligned. And still others gave the illusion of alignment, casting an image of high integrity, but falling short of their own values behind closed doors. I discovered that while most of my clients were successful financially, not all of them were experiencing the same level of personal and professional satisfaction. Some walked in great confidence and peace, while others walked in great anxiety, stress, and regret.

Until they confided in me, they had kept this side of their lives secret, resulting in spiritual, emotional, mental, relational, and even physical stress. Now I want to make it very clear that I never once looked at these leaders with judgment—and still don't to this day. That's just not my style. The very reason I'm able to sit as a "guide" for these individuals is because I respect them so much. However, I had some profound revelations during my first years as a "chief counsel" to these CEOs. The main one being: if misalignment and compromise can happen to great leaders like the ones I admire and serve, it can certainly happen to me!

This revelation sent me on a journey of reconnaissance and discovery that gave birth to this book. *My motivation to go on this journey* was to find a sustainable pattern for healthy living and for leading my *own* path. *My motivation for writing this book* is to share my findings from that personal exploration with the world.

I've witnessed leadership in many forms throughout my life; from my father and mother, to my uncles and aunts, to my iconic high school football coach, Jack Salter, to my Marine Corps commanders and senior enlisted, to spiritual leaders, mentors, and more. Most of these leaders live their life by a code. Some are perfectly aligned with that code, and some are not. My objective in this book is to reveal the patterns and "fruit" of living both aligned and misaligned with your unique character code.

★ ★ ★

My motivation to go on this journey was to find a sustainable pattern for healthy living and for leading my own path. My motivation for writing this book is to share my findings from that personal exploration with the world.

Coach Jack Salter being inducted into the Louisiana High School Coaches Hall of Fame.

My parents and me on my wedding day.

In my opinion, the health of families, organizations, communities, and nations is directly related to the health of their leaders. While my personal moral code is primarily informed by the life of Jesus Christ, and that is what I aspire to reflect, I want to be clear: I certainly haven't arrived (just ask my wife!). I am growing in alignment with my code as a husband, father, and leader, but I still have a long way to go. As a businessperson, I don't have it all figured out yet either. Remember, the best coaches in professional athletics weren't always the best players.

As a coach and counsel to many leaders, I have grown in my ability to listen to and avail myself to wisdom, so I can better support my clients. Like my pastor, Steve Robinson, always says, "We're all in a crock pot cookin' on slow!" That being said, I have discovered a simple yet profound pattern I want to share with you, so let our journey begin!

START WITH THE END IN MIND

When going on a journey, I always start with the end in mind. So let's begin with a brief exercise of reflection. At the time of this writing, it is March of 2020. Many people have died due to the coronavirus pandemic. One of my brothers had the high privilege of sharing a moment with a sick friend before he passed unexpectedly, as a result of contracting the virus. This man was a strong and healthy husband, father, and business owner. His final words to my brother were regarding his family and employees. If he could speak to us from his current dwelling, I am convinced that he would encourage us to LIVE life more richly with others. For him, it was all about relationships. I want to ask you to take a moment and either think about or jot down your answers to the following questions:

If you were witnessing your own funeral, and someone was giving your eulogy, what would you **want** them to say about you? I don't want you to think about what they *would* say at this point; I want you to imagine what you would *want* them to say after you lived a full, rich, and intentionally designed life. What is your definition of a life well lived?

Some categories to consider are:

Category	Your definition of living well
Your spouse & family	
Your faith	
Your work	
Your friendships	
Your finances	
Your life lessons	
Your impact on society	

What is the condition of your relationships? What would be the culmination of your success? How about the work of your hands? How would your life have affected society? Did you maximize your gifts, talents, and abilities on behalf of others, leaving more than you took from the world? Were your days marked by supporting and loving your spouse and children, grandchildren, and even great-grandchildren? Did you pass on the principles and values that made you successful? Did you leave a lasting impact? Or did you just leave resources? These are some questions you can consider as you write your eulogy on the next page.

EULOGY

Date: __________ - __________
Birth Date (Add 90 Years)

Here Lies: ____________________
Full Birth Name

Congratulations! You just joined the ranks of elite leaders who have taken time to reflect upon a life well lived. Studies have shown that less than five percent of the entire population will dare to enter into an exercise like that. But we know there is wisdom in starting with the end in mind.[10]

These are the questions that intrigue enduring leaders. Their ultimate destination determines their daily navigation. As we continue, be encouraged. Though we chart a clear path, there will be storms that can bump us off course. Our success in the end will be: a) who we are becoming on the journey and b) who we help to find success alongside us.

Today, we can forge a sterling character aligned with our unique character code in order to lead and steward well in the Great Transfer of wealth and leadership we find ourselves in.

★ ★ ★

These are the questions that intrigue enduring leaders. Their ultimate destination determines their daily navigation.

[10]"Teach us to number our days that we may gain a heart of wisdom" (Psalm 90:12).

SECTION 3:

CHARACTER PERSONIFIED:

DANIEL'S CONTEXT

ONE OF MY FAVORITE examples of uncompromising character is found in a historical figure who sustained his leadership throughout four different kingdoms and cultures. He kept true to his inner convictions, and therefore was always trusted by top leadership as a chief advisor and steward throughout his entire life. His name was Daniel.

When Daniel was a teenager, his country was invaded and occupied by a foreign government. Part of that nation's strategy was to extract the "best and brightest" individuals from the occupied nation and indoctrinate them into their culture, so they could use those individuals' gifts, talents, and abilities to maintain their control. Daniel (and his friends) stood out, and were selected to serve in the foreign royal court. While serving, Daniel had to manage the tension between the demands of his new king and country, and the

"Daniel in the Lion's Den," Briton Riviere (1872). Oil on canvas.

Photo credit: Walker Art Gallery.

convictions of his own heart, which were oftentimes at odds. Daniel served without compromise, and it's why he was trusted to serve and steward at such high levels of leadership for his entire life.

Just to be clear, living a life true to one's moral code is not always popular, and has historically proven to produce enemies at times. Daniel's jealous rivals attempted to trap him by tricking the king into changing the laws of the land and ultimately sentencing him to death. Unfortunately for those devious rivals, the plan backfired, Daniel was miraculously saved, and the king restored him to his place of influence.

Staying true to your convictions can be scary and uncomfortable in the moment, but in the end, it's always worth it ... and you don't carry the heavy weight of regret!

Daniel's story illustrates how faithfulness to your moral compass must outweigh what others think or even what may happen to you. Daniel could have lived a life of popularity, but instead clung to his convictions, even when his life was on the line. He wasn't always accepted by popular culture—or even admired by his peers—but he was ***respected*** for the level of alignment he had with his moral code, and as a result, he was ***trusted*** to solve the highest issues of the day.

The fruits of living a life of character and integrity are authenticity, confidence, peace of mind, respect, and trust.

Leaders with uncompromising character continue to be called upon for their wisdom and stewardship. That was Daniel—so uncompromising that he was valued by all those he served, regardless of their political agenda or moral code. Here was a man whose leadership spanned different civilizations, societies, and religious constructs. Can you imagine the depth of his wisdom and character?

He was a leader who was truly above reproach.

What you saw was what you got. He was the same in his home as he was in the king's palace—or in our case, standing before the people we lead in business, the president of our company, our employees, the parents of the Little League team we're coaching, or ultimately, our adult children who look to us for guidance and heritage.

Living a life of character and integrity doesn't come naturally, and isn't always easy, but it is always worth it.

"

LIVING A LIFE OF CHARACTER AND INTEGRITY DOESN'T COME NATURALLY AND ISN'T ALWAYS EASY, BUT IT IS ALWAYS WORTH IT."

Daniel was a fallible human being, as we all are, but he demonstrated sterling character throughout his life, always ready to give an account for his actions. Daniel was clear on what his beliefs and convictions were, and used them as a compass to guide his decisions and behaviors. [Later in the book, you will be invited to: a) identify your moral code and b) create your unique Character Code, so that you can live in alignment with both.]

It's important to note that I believe, regardless of your moral code, one can express authentic, confident, fearless leadership. In fact, our culture is drawn to confident leaders from all moral backgrounds. This level of confidence simply comes from living in alignment with one's moral code.

Consider athletes like boxing legend Mike Tyson. As a kid, I used to stand in front of the TV when he walked into the ring, imitating his punches and defeating his opponents with him as I watched. (Oddly enough for my era, I despised video games growing up—but I loved Nintendo's *Mike Tyson's Punch-Out!!* and was the reigning king of Covington, Louisiana!)

Most of us will never know the intense glory and scrutiny of global fame. This level of exposure before the world brings tremendous opportunity for both success and failure, seducing even the best of us. With that being said, I have respect, personally, for anyone who influences on a world stage like Iron Mike. Mike Tyson experienced global acclaim at a very young age, which certainly contributed to the formation of his character and ability to steward his influence. This led him to live his life according to a moral code that may have been different from mine (or yours). However, no one can argue that Iron Mike Tyson isn't authentic, confident, and fearless.

Our admiration for legendary athletes and entertainers, however, is really enshrined in one dimension—their performance in their respective fields of expertise. My point here is this: we love these icons for their ability and contribution to society, but probably wouldn't entrust billion-dollar books of business—or the leadership of our nation—to them. For leaders who want to participate in the Great Transfer, it will require an elevated level of character, integrity, and a life lived above reproach.

The fruit of inspirational leadership is damaged greatly by duplicitous living. My conclusion is that people with a moral code, whether identical to mine or the polar opposite, can influence others in this dynamic, amazing world of 7.8 billion hearts and minds.

However, the rapidly coming era will require leaders to step up their game! Meaning, they will have to live their lives by a standard higher than modern culture, the nation they live in, and the organizations they lead. The most successful, enduring leaders of the next generation may not fit the mold of popular culture. However, like you, they will recognize that they don't have to "fit in" because they were born to "stand out." Legendary leaders like Daniel contributed greatly to their societies, sometimes at their own peril, but these things are certain: their mark has been placed in the history books, their legacies are secure, they lived with no regret, and most importantly, their lives honored the author of their moral code.

Daniel was great because of what he did behind closed doors. It's all too easy, however, to look at highly visible leaders or public figures, see their trappings of success, and imagine that they've made it. There can be a stark difference between who someone presents themselves as, and who they are when no one's watching. As my friend Pastor Randy says, "Either get character, or you'll *become* a character."

CHARACTER VS. CARICATURE

Have you ever been to a carnival or fair and seen the artists who paint quick, comical likenesses of people? A caricature is an exaggerated version of someone or something. In these depictions, the artist will embellish elements of a person's face or body. Maybe they'll make their nose three times its actual size and their chin twice as small. The goal is to create a funny, cartoon image. In leadership, it's possible to have deep, sterling character but also create a *caricature* for marketing purposes. Character embodies who a person genuinely is (based on alignment with their moral code), while a caricature is a created persona designed to sell a product or service.

No one will argue that New Orleans has a loud personality. So, it's no wonder it's a city that loves leaders, entrepreneurs, and artists with over-the-top personalities as well. Growing up, one of NOLA's more visible personalities was the Crawfish King, Al Scramuzza. He owned a popular market called Seafood City—and anyone from our community can sing the jingle from his commercials… "Seafood City is very pretty! Down on Broad and Saint Bernard!"

Al Scramuzza prescribing crawfish as the best medicine!

In these TV spots, a man or a woman would usually get sick, falling down like they'd just had a heart attack, dramatically saying, "I feel bad, I feel bad." Then, Al would rush to their side wearing a white lab coat and stethoscope around his neck, and prescribe the "best medicine" for their ailment: crawfish. He would then give the "sick" person a bite of his famous crawfish and up they would jump, screaming, "I feel good! I feel good!"

On TV, Al was a caricature; an exaggerated version of an enthusiastic market owner. He cast a huge, cartoon-like image for a great marketing effect. Everyone knew who the Crawfish King was—but that didn't mean they actually knew the man behind the caricature. And that's true for each of us.

We each cast a public image (which we'll discuss more deeply in section 6). While it might not be as flamboyant as Al's, we still present a persona to the world. The question is, what's going on behind the scenes?

If we rewind the clock on Al's life, we find him as a kid hanging around seafood stalls in the Great Depression era. His family was struggling to survive, so when loose shrimp and crabs fell off the trucks, he'd scoop them up and take them home. Little Al stood in the gap for his mother and put food on the table, because his father had abandoned them.

Al would later go on to elevate the perception of crawfish as a swamp-bug trash food to an authentic, delicious Southern Louisiana staple. In short, Al Scramuzza made boiled crawfish (available to the general population on demand) famous. But looking behind the commercials and silliness, you find a man who worked hard to care for his family, elevate the culinary scene in his city, and leave a smile on thousands of faces every day.

Al Scramuzza is a great example of quality character behind the shiny caricature. Sure, he wasn't perfect, but he had substance and true desire to make a positive impact on the world. We know this is not always the case. Entire books have been written describing how the "mighty" fall. Or in other words, the caricature is wholly detached from character. So, to participate in this Great Transfer of wealth and leadership, how can we be sure we're more than smoke and mirrors? In the next section, we will attempt to define character, so that we can live our life according to a deep moral code, rather than a temporary caricature, designed to serve our businesses.

SECTION 4:

CHARACTER DEFINED

Character: a person's patterns of speech and behavior over time, shaped by their values, informed by their convictions

SIMPLY PUT, *CHARACTER IS* ***the invisible persona of a visible person***. If a person's moral code is the governing voice in their life, then their character is the defining quality of the invisible dimensions of who they are. Character is both internal and external in nature. A person can sense their character guiding them internally, while others can observe their character through habitual behaviors.

Character can be shaped and refined, which we will talk about in greater detail later in the book. But it rests on the bedrock of our individual moral code. A person's moral code is their internal voice of right and wrong; essentially, it is their **conscience**. For instance, when we are born, it never "initially" feels right to murder another human being. What is that? It is your conscience communicating what is right and wrong.

At some point, a human being begins to accept guidance from forces outside of themself or inside of themself. Outside forces include your family, culture, nation, friends, laws, and more. Inside forces are spiritual in nature. These forces *form* a person's moral code which *informs* their character, and over time, *manifests* into the predictable behaviors and reputation of an individual.

To illustrate this concept in practical terms, imagine you hear something about someone; you will either believe or disbelieve what you heard based on what you've observed in that person's life over a period of time. You would conclude what you heard was either "in character" or "out of character" for this person. What have you been observing? That person's character, informing their behavior, over time.

In summary, character is a person's internal virtues, traits, and reputation made visible over the course of their lifetime. This can be visualized in the following graphic.

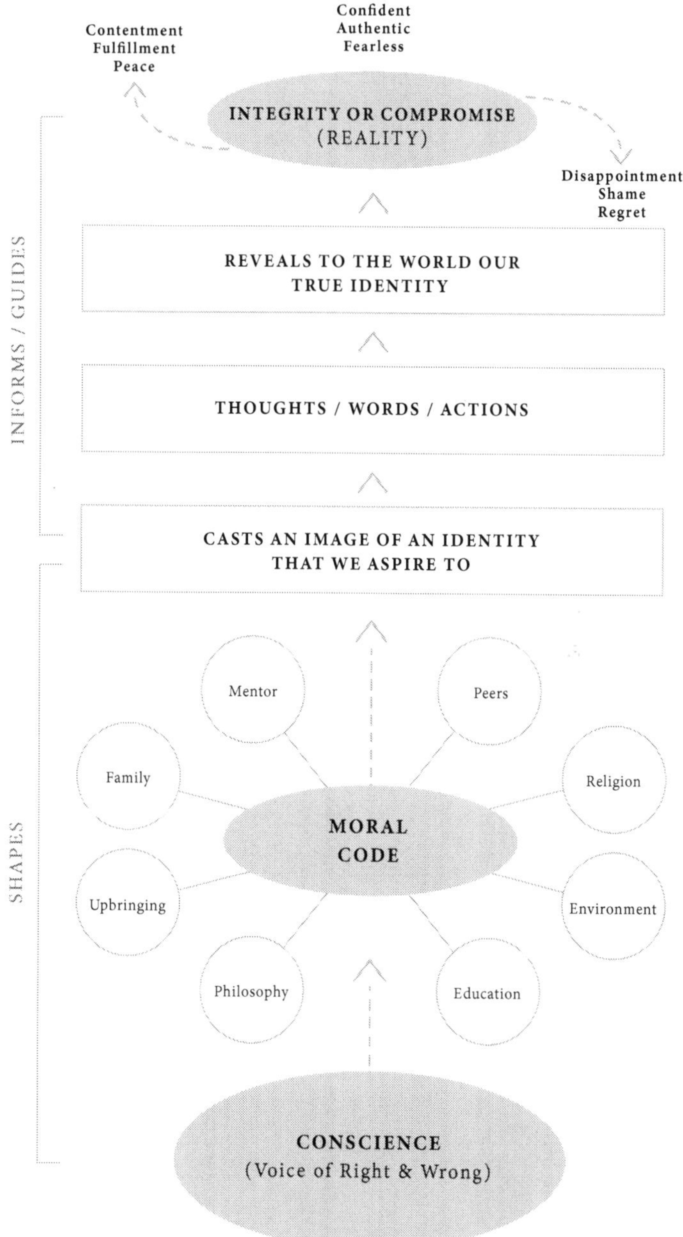
Contentment
Fulfillment
Peace
Confident
Authentic
Fearless
INTEGRITY OR COMPROMISE
(REALITY)
Disappointment
Shame
Regret
INFORMS / GUIDES
REVEALS TO THE WORLD OUR TRUE IDENTITY
THOUGHTS / WORDS / ACTIONS
CASTS AN IMAGE OF AN IDENTITY THAT WE ASPIRE TO
SHAPES
Mentor
Peers
Family
Religion
MORAL CODE
Upbringing
Environment
Philosophy
Education
CONSCIENCE
(Voice of Right & Wrong)

The bedrock of our character is our conscience, or our internal voice of right and wrong. This is the primary driver of our unique, moral code. This code shapes every facet of our lives—from our relationships, to our religion, to the way we raise our children. At the same time, the moral code acts as a projector lens, casting a vision or living image of what kind of person you aspire to be. In turn, this vision informs and guides our thoughts, words, and actions.

The way we show up in the world either corresponds with that image or falls short of it. Regardless, it creates the boundaries in which we live. As time wears on, our thoughts, words, and actions reveal who we really are to the world. Our fundamental identity—or character—is on display. For better or worse, we cannot hide who we are forever. We either live aligned with our conscience, which shapes, guides, and informs everything we are and do, or we live duplicitously. Misalignment causes disappointment, regret, and shame. In fact, the sources of our greatest internal pain often stem directly from living out of sync with our moral code.

Ultimately, I've concluded that leaders must live at a higher level of integrity than the organizations they lead, the people they influence, and even society in general. It begins with listening to that inner voice that is so easy to drown out, and then finding its echoes, as they guide us in our daily actions. This is deep work; it's hard work. But it's the highest value work a leader can do to avoid duplicitous living.

“

THE BEDROCK OF
OUR CHARACTER
IS OUR CONSCIENCE,
OR OUR INTERNAL
VOICE OF RIGHT
AND WRONG.”

SECTION 5:

STANDARDS OF CHARACTER

IF YOU FEEL A pull toward a higher level of character and integrity in this book, that's intentional. You'll hear us calling leaders to a higher standard because the success of our nation (and world) depends on it. While there are multiple layers of standards (e.g., national, social, organizational, familial, personal, etc.), we have seen that the best leaders distinguish themselves *above* all of the others. They live above reproach rather than dancing near the line of transgression that they set for themselves.

Against the backdrop of the Great Transfer, our code of conduct must rise higher than everyone we lead. Our children and grandchildren depend on us to do that. If we don't live this way, we won't even get the torch passed to us—or worse, if we do get it, we run a high risk of snuffing out the flame of success in both our generation and the next.

Now, everything that we've discussed up to this point can be of great benefit to you personally and professionally. However, when it comes to the torch of leadership and stewardship, good character becomes essential because our lack of integrity can either positively or negatively affect others.

The birth of my business, Legendary, represented my leadership torch. It catapulted me onto a national platform, and when I looked at myself in the mirror, I realized that I could easily fumble what had been entrusted to me if I didn't heed the lessons and values I had been taught. This is when I went on a journey to discover a winning pattern of character-based leadership.

My driving question: how do people lead for twenty-five years (or more) without moral, ethical, or financial failures that compromised their values?

This mattered to me because when leaders fail to live at the highest standard, we risk crumbling the interrelated standards that surround us—producing a skeptical, low-trust society.

Let's turn to an example that hits home for me.

NOLA: "THE JEWEL OF THE SOUTH"

As I mentioned before, New Orleans is my home. It's where my people are. I love everything about my city, and in my opinion, New Orleans is the cultural epicenter of the U.S. From our rich history (we just celebrated our tricentennial) to our remarkable

ASTOR
GATEWAY

diversity of people, food, music, and art, it's hard to beat this amazing place. As a child, I saw the richness and **innocence of our community**. We used to visit my grandfather (Papa Songy) during the summers. When the time was right, he would say, "okay, kiddos—hop in!" which meant we were going to City Park to get ice cream. He would load all of the cousins up in his suburban,

pop in a Louis Armstrong tape, light up his pipe, and off we went. City Park and Storyland was a kid's dream. We used to climb the live oaks, feed the ducks, paddle boat down the canals, and get ice cream from the casino. After all of that, we would take a train ride around the park and try and squeeze in a carousel ride.

As a young man, I saw a different side of NOLA. I began to see the **mischievous side** to my beloved city. Bourbon Street, Pat O'Brien's, Mardi Gras, night clubs, and raves... The city never lacked for good times or parties. I can remember going to a Mardi Gras Ball after-party when I was in high school, thinking, *I wonder if any of this is legal?*

It wasn't until I became an adult that I started seeing the **shady or corrupt** side of our community. This ancient port city bears the burden of a dark history, revealed and redeemed most recently after one of our greatest tragedies—Hurricane Katrina.

Famous Bourbon Street at night in the French Quarter.

Growing up, I witnessed corruption eroding the city's foundations. New Orleans has lost out on a staggering number of lucrative business opportunities in the past, simply because its reputation was tarnished by consistent, deliberate corruption. And it wasn't exclusive to one sector of our community. Corruption permeated politics, business, ministry, nonprofits, arts and entertainment, and education.

Healthy businesses simply do not invest in unhealthy communities.

That being said, I *love* how New Orleans sees herself. We are the only city that I am aware of whose emblem is a church (the St. Louis Cathedral), whose NFL football team is the Saints, and who is

St. Louis Cathedral.

proudly represented by the fleur-de-lis (a symbol of the Holy Trinity). New Orleans projects an image of faith, family, and rich culture at her core. I believe that she is beautiful. However, she is also known as a place where people come and do things that they would never do in their hometown. If you want to do business or move your headquarters here, you need to "kiss the ring" or pay off the right person. Corrupt practices like these are what deter opportunities, force our sons and daughters to look to other states and countries for employment, and ultimately, rob our city of her greatness and destiny.

And then Hurricane Katrina hit.

As one of the largest natural disasters in modern times, Hurricane Katrina changed everything. It was late summer of 2005 and the Category Five hurricane pulverized the region, causing nearly twenty-three breaches in the drainage canal and navigational canal levees and floodwalls in New Orleans alone. By the third day, eighty percent of the city was flooded, with some parts under fifteen feet of water. Nearly ninety percent of the residents evacuated, and thousands took shelter in the Louisiana Superdome.

But Hurricane Katrina did more than physically damage New Orleans. It swept across our community in a way that laid bare the corruption that haunted the city for so long. As billions of dollars poured in to help with recovery efforts, it was followed by the eyes of the nation, exposing a vacuum of leaders who, in some cases, did not properly steward the resources.

"IF THERE'S ONE THING ABOUT CHARACTER, IT'S THAT REDEMPTION IS ONLY ONE DECISION AWAY."

An aerial view from a United States Navy helicopter showing floodwaters around the Louisiana Superdome (stadium) and surrounding area (2005).

Image courtesy of United States Navy.

A laundry list of local elected officials, businesspeople, and nonprofit leaders were called out for mismanagement, poor communication, and corruption. In fact, there are major players who lost their seats of leadership for their involvement in these activities, some of whom are still paying the price currently. Why? Because their thoughts, motives, and actions weren't aligned with either their own moral code or the civil moral code of the land.

Hurricane Katrina was a "cleansing" of sorts. It shook the pillars of New Orleans society, and tested the resolve and the fortitude of over a million citizens. And through the rebuilding effort, we are seeing the rise of quality, above-reproach leaders who, in large part, demonstrate solid character and clearly understand how much is at stake.

If there's one thing about character, it's that redemption is only one decision away. And that one good decision leads to another. Hurricane Katrina was a catalyst for change, a chance to take an honest look at what we wanted our legacy to be, and to build it on something sturdy, honest, and good.

New Orleans will continue to rise. Right now, we're walking in a redemptive story. Katrina forced our hand—we started operating at a higher standard. It's going to take some time, but as leaders practice high integrity, and more importantly, hold others to that same standard, our progress will shape future generations.

Simply put, character and integrity foster trust and are very attractive to opportunity. In my opinion, together, they form one of our greatest advantages.

SECTION 6:

CHARACTER AS AN ADVANTAGE:

THE PANEL

WHEN I STARTED MY CONSULTING business, I remember having dinner with my pastor, discussing this new opportunity. He said, "Phil, know this, everybody has a public life, a private life, and a secret life. It's your job to help them find harmony between the three dimensions of their lives and their core convictions."

The concept of the three dimensions rang true as a realization dawned on me: *if I am going to inspire people to maximize their life, leadership, and legacy, I would have to have a proven pattern for healthy living, and it would have to start with me.* This started a journey of discovery to learn the best practices of leaders with impeccable stewardship.

The mission was simple: learn from a panel of the best and brightest about how they sustained leadership success over the course of their careers, so that I could help myself, my family, and my clients.

I assembled a research team and created a set of criteria. I started by dividing society into seven pillars: business, government, ministry, education, arts and entertainment, athletics, and military.

Our criteria were that members of the panel led at the highest levels for twenty-five years (or more) and served without any moral, ethical, or financial failures that removed them from their leadership position. It didn't mean we searched for the "perfect" leaders. (There are none, in my opinion.) Instead, we wanted to study leaders who had maintained the highest standards of uncompromising character in all three dimensions of their life. (We will outline these dimensions in the pages ahead.)

So, who are these leaders? While we have agreed to keep their names confidential, we can share their sphere and level of leadership. These are some of our leaders' offices and categories:

1. Founder/CEO of a billion dollar national company
2. United States Marine Corps Lieutenant General
3. United States Congressman
4. Senior Pastor of a multi-site church
5. International movement (non-profit) minister
6. United States Senator
7. Arts and Entertainment Celebrity
8. Hollywood Actor

9. Hired CEO of $500,000,000 national company
10. Education Chief
11. Non-Governmental Organization Chief
12. Professional Athlete

Through these interviews, we discovered trends and patterns of successful living we can all learn from.

This being said, as I began to write this book, laying out these positive (and even inspiring) case studies, I was challenged by a leader in South Africa to broaden our research sample. He suggested that I also include those who had failed morally, ethically, or financially, and then been reinstated. I took his advice—and discovered an amazing thing. Those who faithfully followed the pattern sustained their leadership without fumbling the torch. In contrast, those who disregarded the pattern failed in ways that removed them from their seat.

This pattern works in both directions: sustaining and losing leadership positions.

For those who fell and were reinstated, the story is arguably more beautiful. The nature of our humanity is that it's fallible. Meaning that all of us will experience failure and misalignment during our lives. But I have good news, there is life after failure. It's about trying again with wisdom. Remember the oyster shells. Dust off. Get back up. Keep rolling. Your leadership matters.

“

EVERY PERSON—
LEADER OR NOT—
HAS A PUBLIC,
PRIVATE, AND
SECRET LIFE.”

As I expose our findings, I will keep names private, not only to honor our confidentiality agreements, but also because my desire is not to *call people out*, but to *call people up*. So far, everything you have read has been history, context, or my opinion. From this point forward, I will share the research, include real-life accounts of these leaders, and provide an actionable framework you can use to apply this pattern positively to sustain your life, leadership, and legacy.

Here is what we found.

THE THREE DIMENSIONS OF A LEADER

Every person—leader or not—has a public, private, and secret life. Like an iceberg floating in the sea, sunlight shines brightly on everything above the waterline (representing our public life). As the sunlight filters through the water, its illuminating power diminishes, until finally, the water fades to inky black. This is the transition from your private life to your secret life. Our public life is fully visible, our private life is somewhat visible, and many of our secret lives are completely invisible to others.

PUBLIC LIFE

Your public life includes anything in the public eye—whether it's your vocation, serving on a board, coaching a team, or stewarding resources that affect others. If you are in leadership, you automatically have eyes on what you do in public. This is your life on display.

Anytime there are multiple sets of eyes on your decisions and actions, other than your family's, chances are that is your public expression.

Even if part of your life is shielded from the eye of the general public, if it can be seen, it's technically public and open for scrutiny. You could be leading a publicly traded company, coaching a Little League team, serving at a local food shelter, teaching a class at church, or leading the local 5K run. It's on the record; it's available; it's public.

PRIVATE LIFE

Your private life includes your spouse, your children, your extended family, and your close, personal friendships. It's the stuff of weekend card games, trips with fishing and hunting buddies, conversations in book clubs, dance conventions, and more. This is your "nonworking" life. Outside of our family, my dad's private life consisted of a coffee crew, a lunch crew, a tennis crew, and a card crew. You have this dimension, too.

Let's be honest, in the age of technology and disruption, our private lives are not so private anymore. For example, I was standing in our home one evening, reprimanding my son about how he had just spoken to his mother, when I noticed my daughter's phone in her hand. As I looked more closely, I saw a little face staring back at me with a horrified look. My daughter was FaceTiming with one of her friends who overheard my entire intense conversation with my son. Let's just say it was a sobering moment for me. In my embarrassment,

I said, "Are you FaceTiming someone?!" To which the girl on the phone responded, "Bye, Mr. Phil!" and hung up abruptly.

Technology and social media have provided wonderful new avenues to communicate with each other. However, they have also opened windows and doors, allowing others to see into our private lives.

SECRET LIFE

Finally, let's discuss the concept of a secret life. Now, I know that this sounds dark and mysterious (which is the reason I chose it as the title of this book!). Some people argue that if you really are a person of integrity, you shouldn't have a secret life. I disagree. Plenty of good, wonderful things happen in secret. For instance, some of the most incredibly generous people I know give privately, without another soul ever knowing. Some people are deeply religious and keep that part of their lives secret as well.

Some of us journal and write letters in our secret lives. The day before my father's funeral, my brother and I found a letter that my father wrote, addressed to his children, to be read at his death. When we opened it, we discovered that it was dated July 29, 1981. It had been sealed for thirty-three years. It was a beautiful, kind sentiment that he guarded with secrecy while he was alive.

While I've never shared the image of my father's letter before, I've read it to tens-of-thousands of people on three separate continents. This was a noble act in his secret life that benefited us greatly and continues to benefit countless others.

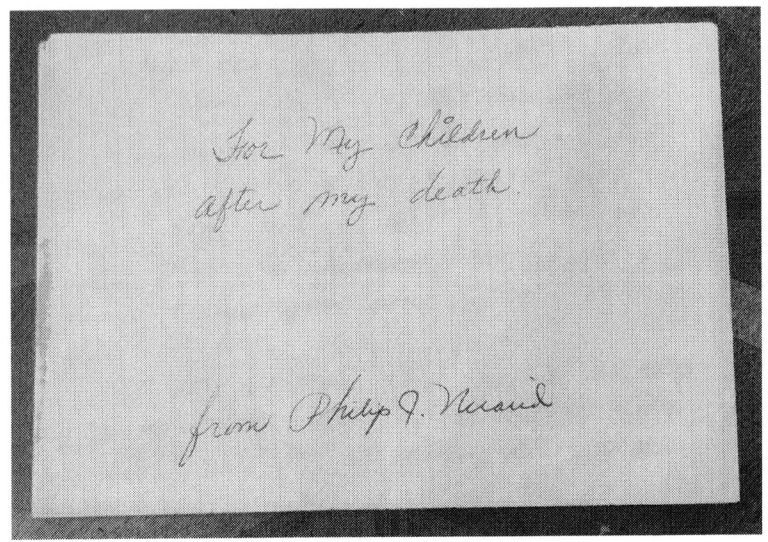

For My Children
after my death.

from Philip J. Nicaud

[I debated on whether or not to share the image of my father's letter with you because it's so personal. But as a leader, I've learned to push through personal discomfort for the benefit of others.]

To My Children, 7-29-81 1:00 AM
(Shane, Philip Jr, Matthew, Amy, + Louis)

I would like to say that I love each of you in a very special way.

I hope one day that each of you will find the happiness that I have found living with your mother and each of you.

I am writing this letter because I hope that each of you would like to know why (in my opinion) all of us were put on this earth. The answer is to get to God. (our creator) Since there are five of you there may be five different ways, (or roads), for each of you to choose. Which road is not as important but remember you must go through Jesus Christ. He is our Savior. No one else. I hope by the time this is read

– over –

A little "hello"

©AG

EACH OF YOU WILL HAVE BEEN INTRODUCED TO CHRIST IN A SPECIAL WAY. MY INTRODUCTION WAS SPECIAL BECAUSE YOUR MOTHER PLAYED A VERY BIG PART IN MY COMING to BELIEVE IN JESUS CHRIST AS OUR SAVIOR.

REMEMBER, WHEN TIMES ARE HARD THAT CHRIST WILL BE WITH YOU EVEN THOUGH I CAN'T.

YOUR MOTHER AND I BUILT OUR LIVES ON A THEORY THAT WENT SOMETHING LIKE THIS. WHEN TIMES ARE HARD AND THINGS SEEM to BE AT THIER WORST WE MUST RISE to the OCCASSION, AND TAKE ONE STEP AT A TIME. THINGS LOOK BAD WHEN ONE VIEWS the OVERALL PICTURE. TAKE THINGS ONE STEP AT A TIME AND EVERY THING WILL WORK OUT IN THE END. IN OTHER WORDS WHEN ITS TIME to EAT, EAT, WHEN ITS TIME TO PLAY, PLAY, AND WHEN ITS TIME to WORK, WORK! IN THIS MANNER WE CONTINUE TO MOVE ALONG TOWARD OUR EVENTUAL DESTINATION. "THE LORD" I LOVE YOU MY CHILDREN. GOD BLESS YOU ALL! Daddy.

Wow. My brother and I were a puddle on the floor after reading that letter. But that one act, done in secret by my father, has not only inspired me to conduct my life at a higher standard, but it has also served as a guide to lead people to write their own eulogies at all of my conferences over the years.

There are plenty of noble things done in secret or behind the scenes; things done in faith, sacrifice, generosity, or service, that no one will ever know about. However, we also experience struggle in secret sometimes, and that's okay. Sometimes you need to grow in an area, but you don't need to broadcast that to the world. For example, if your business is going through challenging times, it is wise to carefully select the people you choose to discuss it with. In one sense, it is unfair to dump heavy leadership weight on some of your close relationships that are not designed to carry it. In another case, it would be unwise to include a third party, unless they could serve as part of the solution to that challenge.

If each of these areas of your life is aligned with your moral code, exposure wouldn't damage you or the people around you. Your secret life only becomes dangerous when you harbor a secret that goes against your core convictions or moral code. If it could hurt you, your family, your business, or others, it could be a dark area of your secret life that may lead to massive regret.

The good things we do in secret—our faith, good deeds, giving, and so on—give us rest. They encourage us. They reset our souls, and remind us of what is important. They provide strength. But I'm here to tell you, friends, a dark secret life will do the exact opposite. A dark secret life is a recipe for massive battery drain. Symptoms such as anxiety, paranoia, bursts of anger, mental anguish, and many more accompany this practice.[11] A dark secret life seldom destroys you from the outside … but rather from the inside. I'm not being dramatic; I'm being honest.

A dark secret life can cause great regret because whatever you did (or didn't do) violated your conscience. This is how a dark secret life begins. You do something "out of character" that violates your moral code. You knew it at the time, and you know it now. It doesn't line up with what you know is right. It wasn't your original intention, but the damage is done, and because of your leadership position, you can't see how you could tell anyone (you lack exposure). Your public clout has reached such a level that if you do tell someone, there could be massive consequences for you and others. Your reputation could be tarnished, your stakeholders may lose value, your business partners might become hostile, you could lose the respect of your employees or team, and your family could be deeply wounded. The consequences are real, and the stakes are high.

At this stage, you feel stuck, leveraged, and the secrets (or fear) that you carry begin to oppress and drain you. Your ego takes over, and like a magnet, you're pulled back to whatever temptation or indiscretion got you there in the first place. You get away with it. Again and again. But now it becomes a pattern of unhealthy, misaligned living and leading.

---

[11]Slepian, M.L., Chun, J.S., & Mason, M.F. (2017). The experience of secrecy. *Journal of Personality and Social Psychology*, 113(1), 1–33. https://doi.org/10.1037/pspa0000085.

The end to this story is never good. There are three ways that a dark secret life plays out.

1. **The secret remains a secret until you die, causing:**
    a. Trauma to your identity (you become someone you are not proud of)
    b. Trauma to your emotional and psychological well-being
    c. Trauma to your legacy (if or when it is discovered after you die)
2. **The secret gets exposed while you're living, causing:**
    a. Trauma to yourself (fractured mental and emotional well-being)
    b. Trauma to others (fractured relationships)
    c. Trauma to your lifestyle and/or freedom (fractured heritage and legacy)
3. **The secret is exposed in a controlled manner while you're living, causing:**
    a. The trauma to be calculated and orchestrated in a confidential way

While we admit that there is risk in exposing a dark secret life, our research shows that the benefits of transparency in a confidential and controlled manner far outweigh the risk of the other methods of exposure. If you don't believe us, consider the study from Harvard researchers that concluded secret-keeping comes with significant cost to your health and well-being—with the potential of shortening your life.[12]

Integrity among the dimensions of our public, private, and secret lives authenticates who we are before the watching world. This causes us to be confident and fearless, and live life with no regret. The call to a higher level of stewardship, however, requires a higher level of intentionality.

The leaders we researched understood this, and possessed a unique posture (mindset) and process (strategy) that guided their lives and gave them a distinct advantage. We call this discovery the *EPA Advantage*.

[12]Slepian, Chun, & Mason, The experience of secrecy, 1–33.

SECTION 7:

THE EPA ADVANTAGE

The Winning Formula

THE PATTERN WE DISCOVERED is simple. The enduring leaders we studied had high degrees of exposure, perspective, and accountability in all three dimensions of their lives—we call this the *EPA Advantage*. I will now define each element of this winning formula, so we have a baseline of understanding.

EXPOSURE

[Second-Party Transparency]

The first element of living with integrity in all dimensions of your life is exposure, or transparency, which is grounded in sight.

The way you know if you have exposure in any area of your life is whether or not you have other sets of eyes on it. Question: who has complete vantage into every area of your life? The first thing I learned on my journey was to increase my level of exposure. Personally, I make it a practice to expose each layer of my life to people I trust or am in a contractual, confidential relationship with. It means they have controlled, limited access bound by the various dimensions of my life.

The trend I saw in successful leaders' finances, for example, was that many had multiple sets of eyes on every dollar they earned and spent. From their CFO to their personal bookkeeper, their CPA, and their spouses, many people could view their accounts and credit card activity. The only way they could hide spending activity was through petty cash, but they had also given all the "sets of eyes" permission to ask them about those funds. It's important to note that any system can be tricked. In other words, you can get away with anything if you put your mind to it. However, these leaders set their exposure to such a high degree that it would be very difficult for them to spend money on anything that would violate their values.

Finances are just one area. The majority of our case studies had others' eyes on their calendar, social media, emails, business and personal connections, and even travel. Most had a code of conduct for how they transparently interact with people. Exposure means having witnesses—and witnesses create transparency and breed protection for all parties.

PERSPECTIVE

[Second-Party Counsel]

The second element of living with integrity in all dimensions of your life is perspective. I'll illustrate this by drawing your attention to the military and how modern warfare is waged. When I served in the United States Marine Corps in the early '90s, we had limited perspective of the battlefield. We relied heavily on intelligence, reconnaissance, and forward observation reporting. Today, our troops have a massive advantage. Remote-controlled drone aircraft afford ground troops a 30,000-foot view of the entire battlefield in high-definition. This gives our military a broader perspective in developing the strategies to win not only the battle, but the war. Perspective is a major advantage—and you can gain that advantage through a person who has a "higher vantage point" on your life and leadership.

We discovered that our case studies had a host of "input" relationships that crowned their lives with wisdom. Some of these advisors included: boards, mentors, consultants, coaches, pastors, and all of the various professional advisors you would expect in a leader's life. From our research, these advisors can be divided into two categories: contractual and non-contractual. An interesting fact is that currency was used to procure both of these perspectives. Financial currency was used for contractual relationships; honor and relational currency for non-contractual relationships.

At the end of the day, when you seek a higher perspective, that means you possess the humility to avail yourself to lifted counsel.

It's in our nature to be independent, but sometimes when we make decisions without another perspective, we risk not seeing a situation from every angle. Virtually all of the leaders we studied possessed a wealth of trusted counsel that they drew from. Wise advisors can provide safety and guidance that give us an advantage in our life and leadership.[13]

ACCOUNTABILITY

[Second-Party Action Management]

The third element of living with integrity in all dimensions of your life is accountability. In our business, we teach four dimensions of accountability. After our clients design their personal and professional master plan, we coach them in the following four actions of accountability:

1. Write it down.
2. Speak it to other people.
3. Review it frequently.
4. Invite another human being to ask you about it with regular frequency.

The primary accountability factor that we identified while interviewing the panel of leaders is that they all had a high degree of

[13]"For by wise counsel you will wage your own war, and in a multitude of counselors there is safety" (Proverbs 24:6).

invited human accountability. In our opinion, this is one of the highest forms of accountability. That being said, if invited human accountability is giving leaders the greatest advantage in achieving their desired outcomes, then we can conclude that great, sustainable leadership is primarily about relationships.

Accountability gets a bad rap. We associate it with having to check in with someone who can tell us if we're getting it right. But what if we thought about accountability in a different light? What if we associated accountability with freedom?

To me, exposure, perspective, and accountability are like the world-renowned sport of bumper bowling. It's almost impossible for your bowling ball to go into the gutter because it's guarded by bumpers along the entire lane ... The difference is that in life, you get to choose what the "bumpers" look like! The guardrails of life don't keep you from your best; they ensure that you reach your highest potential.

BAND OF BROTHERS

About sixteen years ago, I was invited to attend a Wednesday morning men's breakfast. I'll never forget the speaker, Pastor Dave, who gave a message that I'd never heard before on Lordship and repentance. Essentially, he called out duplicitous living, but admitted that apart from the grace of God, it is impossible to live in perfect alignment with your convictions. There was obvious health and vibrancy in every layer of his life: public, private, and secret. However, he was still open and honest about his struggles. Yet, somehow, this *vulnerability* added to his *credibility*.

I didn't know it at the time, but his message, coupled with the group dynamic afterwards, introduced me to the *EPA Advantage*. Each Wednesday morning we met to discuss areas of alignment and misalignment with our core convictions. We invited perspective and held ourselves to a standard of shared accountability. In the process, this band of brothers provided weekly encouragement and fuel for the journey.

The incredible growth we experienced was the result of the *EPA Advantage* that works every time. I have discovered that people with totally different religious and moral identifications live this way as well. It works because they put an equal amount of distrust in their own ability to live life in sync with their core convictions.

Some examples that come to mind are the concept of organizations like Vistage, YPO, Convene, C12, and more. These CEO roundtable groups prove that this model is effective in providing lifted exposure, perspective, and accountability to reach our highest potential.

The trick is finding the right people to invite into your circle of trust—which we turn to now.

SECTION 8:

RELATIONSHIPS

★ ★ ★

IN 2004, THE OAK was designated as America's national tree, a symbol of the nation's strength and steady growth.

As a child, I took a trip to Mandeville, Louisiana (where I currently live) to wrap my arms around the largest certified live oak tree in North America. It's called the Seven Sisters Oak, a nod to its former owner, who was one of seven sisters.

Tourists flock to see the Seven Sisters Oak each year, collecting fallen acorns and leathery leaves, and snapping pictures in the shade of her limbs, which stretch 139 feet from tip to tip. It towers above neighborhood homes at sixty-eight feet. This tree is big, and it's impressive. But do you know what is more impressive than this single oak tree? Gazing upon an entire grove of majestic oaks, looking as if they are standing in formation.

The Seven Sisters Oak tree.

As mentioned before, I grew up near the iconic City Park in New Orleans, Louisiana. The park boasts over 1,300 acres of oak groves, buildings, bridges, streams, and ponds. City Park was loaded with live oak groves that we would climb and swing from, fearless and free.

As mighty and majestic as oak trees are, surprisingly, they don't have deep roots. Their roots run shallow and wide, and in an oak grove, they will actually intertwine with the roots of other trees to provide additional strength and support.

The arms of a standalone oak will grow to the ground, the weight of its massive limbs too much to bear. But in contrast, the limbs of the trees in a grove will grow upward, reaching toward the warmth and light of the sun. The closer the trees are, the more they reach

Oak grove in New Orleans City Park.

Image courtesy of City of New Orleans.

upward. The tangle of the roots and the competition for light creates a healthy tension—each tree equally and structurally balanced.

The greatest strength of the grove? The trees become like a single organism through an interconnected root system. If one tree is under stress, they are all under attack, and will resist with chemical compounds to fight off bacteria, fungi, carpenter ants, and spiders.[14]

The analogy to our life and leadership is clear—we are better together!

---

[14]Moniz, William A. "Arborist Explains Oak Grove Ecosystem." *Southcoasttoday.com*, Southcoasttoday.com, 17 Sept. 2009, www.southcoasttoday.com/article/20090917/PUB03/909170374.

"

ISOLATION TRULY IS AN ENEMY TO OUR HEALTH AS LEADERS."

Creating a grove is like linking arms with your friends and family, your support system, your mentors and coaches. Isolation truly is an enemy to our health as leaders. And like an oak grove, we are stronger and more enduring when we invest in relationships in three areas: input, neutral, and output.

INPUT RELATIONSHIPS

As I discussed at a high level in the section on perspective, input relationships are key to a fully integrous life. In fact, the majority of people I interviewed had a cabinet of sorts, a board of advisors, or a looser network of key relationships; people who advised them both professionally and personally. Of course, they had the essential accountants, lawyers, tax advisors, and wealth managers. But additionally, almost all of them had a spiritual voice—a pastor, priest, or rabbi. Another input relationship we identified were mentors. (Many cited being mentored through reading books, as well.)

We noticed an interesting trend when studying these relationships: many leaders didn't have the time to develop the level of trusting relationships that it takes to be so vulnerable, so they would hire them out.

If they didn't have the time to develop a trusting input relationship organically, they would bind a professional in confidentiality, and utilize them to process their life and leadership decisions.

Some hired input relationships that are worth noting are advisors such as executive coaches, wealth managers, a board of advisors, etc.

Everyone we interviewed had seen a therapist or counselor, either currently or in the past. Membership in noncompetitive peer leadership groups (e.g., Vistage, YPO, C12, Convene, 20 Groups, etc.) was also a common trend. These input relationships consistently provided exposure, perspective, and accountability.

NEUTRAL RELATIONSHIPS

If you've given up on the idea of true friendships (neutral relationships), we'd love for you to consider reassessing that area of your life. One of the greatest blessings in life is a true friend.

There's a science to the success of neutral relationships. A twenty-year study from Harvard Medical School and the University of California, San Jose found that happiness is "a collective phenomenon that spreads through social networks like an emotional contagion."[15] Nearly five thousand individuals were studied for two decades. During this time, researchers found that one person's happiness "triggers a chain reaction" that benefits everyone in their relational network—starting with their friends. Even better, this effect lasts up to one year.

I can say with both scientific and experiential authority that genuine friendships offer some of the greatest joys of life. Perhaps business or power has polluted your neutral friendships? Perhaps you're the

---

[15]Cameron, David. "Having Happy Friends Can Make You Happy." Harvard Gazette, 5 Dec. 2008, news.harvard.edu/gazette/story/2008/12/having-happy-friends-can-make-you-happy/.

influencer of every relationship in your world? This is common for people with a propensity toward leadership, so don't beat yourself up or think that you're failing.

Most of the people we interviewed (and many of you reading this book) are always "on duty" or "have to be somebody." In other words, you're always operating in your leadership gifts. While we all can enjoy a lifted perspective from input relationships, neutral relationships provide a safe place for us to be "off duty." A surprising trend that we discovered is that many of the people we interviewed, and most of the leaders I'm involved with in business, have a large number of acquaintances, but very few close personal friends. However, they did recognize the importance of having a small group of intimate, neutral friendships; people with whom they could "turn off," relax, and have fun with.

Consider how Bill Gates answered the question, "What is your idea of success?" He cited his friend and billionaire investor, Warren Buffet, saying, "... the greatest measure of success is whether the people close to you are happy and love you."[16] Expounding on this lesson in a separate article, Gates said, "I've learned many things from Warren over the last twenty-five years, but maybe the most important thing is what friendship is all about. It's about being the kind of friend you wish you had yourself."[17]

---

[16]Schwantes, Marcel. "Bill Gates Says He Now Asks Himself 1 Crucial Question He Would Not Have Asked in His Microsoft Days." Inc.com, Inc., 6 Apr. 2020, www.inc.com/marcel-schwantes/bill-gates-says-he-now-asks-himself-1-crucial-question-he-would-not-have-asked-in-his-microsoft-days.html.

[17]Gates, Bill. "25 Years of Learning and Laughter." Gatesnotes.com, Bill Gates, 5 July 2016, www.gatesnotes.com/About-Bill-Gates/25-Years-of-Learning-and-Laughter.

Leadership can be lonely at times. I'm sorry to say that. However, it doesn't have to be all of the time. The key is to seek common interests. Remember this: common interests and shared values breed intimacy. We've seen this play out in two groups of neutral relationships: pre-leadership and post-leadership friends.

Pre-Leadership Neutral Relationships

One interesting insight we discovered is that most of our panel valued friendships with others who knew them prior to their success. For example, old high school and college friends, military buddies, former teammates, and so on. We tend to find it refreshing to be around people who know us; there's no ulterior motive and they keep us rooted. But ... the reality is some of those close relationships can become a drain if there is massive misalignment in current means, values, or common interests. I want to be clear that these neutral relationships can certainly be beneficial. However, in our experience, healthy expectations and boundaries should be visited to keep the relationship mutually beneficial.

Post-Leadership Neutral Relationships

It's important to seek peer relationships where you have common interests and values. As we said before, shared values and common interests breed intimacy. Some healthy categories to consider are people who have common means, values, and mindsets. Take a moment and make a list of the neutral relationships that you have (or want to have). In this exercise, ask yourself some questions using the following criteria. Consider the grid to see more clearly which neutral relationships to invest in.

Category	**Johnny** *Existing Friend*	**Jane** *Existing Friend*	**Juan** *New Friend*
Common Interests (Hobbies)	☑ Golfer	☑ Tennis player	☑ Hunter
Common Means (Financial)		☑ Similar financial means	☑ Similar financial means, time, and freedom
Common Values (Faith, Family, Etc.)	☑ Faith & Family	☑ Faith & Family	☑ Faith & Family
Common Mindset (Leadership, Growth, Etc.)		☑ Quality leader	☑ Invests in personal growth

The waters of life and leadership can be peaceful in one moment and raging in another. But let me conclude by saying there's nothing like a true friend to help you navigate all the waters of life.

OUTPUT RELATIONSHIPS

Finally, we found that the leaders we studied had relationships with people they were pouring into as well. We call these "output relationships." These included people they were mentoring, coaching, or teaching. It's important to note that not all of them were one-on-one mentoring relationships. Many of these leaders hosted group coaching or mentoring sessions. The key is simply that they helped promising people go further, faster.

Personally, I was curious as to the selection process of the people they mentored. The trending criteria that I discovered was that the mentees were humble, hungry, and honoring. Humble—in other words, if they were prideful or arrogant, no one wanted to invest in them. Hungry—if the leaders had to push them to use the time wisely rather than being eagerly asked questions, it wasn't a good investment for the leader. Lastly, honoring—the mentees treated these leaders with tremendous respect. An easy way to understand honor is by looking at the definition of dishonor: to treat in a degrading manner. Or put another way, to treat something or someone *special* as *ordinary*.

It's a privilege to be mentored by seasoned, successful, high-integrity leaders. It's also a joy to mentor the humble, hungry, and honoring generation who are coming into their own. These relationships have a mutually beneficial effect: joy for the mentor, growth for the mentee.

Finally, here's a surprising benefit of output relationships we uncovered. If you want to grow in your understanding of certain areas or topics, it may be time to teach them. I believe the learning process is never completed until you give it away. Once you give knowledge away, you become its author—meaning you understand it far more deeply. And naturally, this process of giving increases the level of accountability you have for the information and how you apply it yourself. If you don't give it away, you'll never experience that depth of accountability. So, mentoring, coaching, and teaching are as much for you as they are for the person being taught or mentored. And that is the power of output relationships.

CONCLUDING THOUGHTS ON RELATIONSHIPS

In summary, it can be lonely at the top. Our lives were not meant to be like the Seven Sisters Oak—grand but alone. We're designed to function best in the context of healthy input, neutral, and output relationships.

In my experience, there are a host of reasons why people avoid the vulnerability (and potential trauma) that accompany authentic relationships. There may have been past attempts at building relationships that led to failure, betrayal, being taken advantage of, or neglect over time. Others have experienced real physical, sexual, or verbal abuse resulting in tremendous mental and emotional stress, fracturing their ability to trust. These unhealthy scenarios create understandable barriers for people, causing reluctance to trust again and re-enter into healthy neutral relationships.

I'm not minimizing any of the pain associated with unhealthy relational trauma. Relationships can certainly be complicated and messy—and I know there are valid hurts and disappointments that we all have experienced. But if, after reading this, you're convinced it's time to give healthy relationships another shot, I want to commend you.

We've taken the road opposite of isolation, because in our research and opinion, isolation leads to a dark kind of self-talk, and could ultimately lead to self-sabotage and great regret.

I want to conclude this section on relationships with a story from my personal life. My father and I didn't have the best relationship in my thirties. After much reflection, I believe that my father, like many of us—myself included at times—struggled with the disappointments of life, the consequences of poor choices, the natural decline of his health, and to be quite honest, his own mortality. This caused widespread trauma in many of his closest relationships.

During this time, both my pastor, Steve Robinson, as well as a friend of mine, Troy Duhon, told me about a man named Daniel Harkavy and an event he and his team hosted on the West Coast called the Building Champions Experience. On their recommendation, my friend Kenny and I attended this event. In Daniel's opening comments, he said, "If you don't like a key relationship in your life, you can do something about it."

When I heard him say that, I thought, *Yeah, but it takes two to tango.* No sooner did those words hit my mind than Daniel said aloud, "I know that it takes two to tango!" I looked around the room at over five hundred leaders and thought to myself, *Did I just say that with my mouth?!* Needless to say, the timing of his words with my thoughts grabbed my attention.

Daniel went on to explain that, "Relationships matter, and you have more influence over the quality of them than you realize. You can design the future that you desire. All it takes is a documented vision and intentional plan to get that future. If the relationship reconciles, you've won greatly. If it doesn't, at least you've communicated your willingness to try, exhausted all that you can do, and lived life with no regret."

I received his encouragement hook, line, and sinker, did exactly what he prescribed, and through this process, my relationship with my father was restored within six months. Little did I know that within two years, I would find him dead of a heart attack one summer afternoon. I can't tell you how grateful I am to my pastor and friend for connecting me with Daniel Harkavy, and for Daniel himself, who had the courage to set a room of leaders on the course of intentional living and relational reconciliation.

Relationships can be difficult to develop and maintain, but they can also be an incredible joy and your greatest advantage. If you are to maximize your potential, healthy relationships are simply a part of the process. May we all have the courage to fight the good fight of relational health.

THE MANHOOD CEREMONY

Naturally, I'm a highly relational guy. (My DiSC looks like a slide on a playground: ninety-four percent D, one hundred percent I, and then S and C on the floor!) People energize me, so I've always valued being around them. While I'm competitive and like to win, I see relationship building as my number one strength—and so I wanted to pass this on to my children as well.

The Manhood Ceremony in the Legendary Leadership Consultants boardroom.

Years ago, I read a book by Robert Lewis called *Raising a Modern Day Knight*. This is one of the most profound books I've read on the topic of raising sons. About two years ago, I invited ten of my son's (Little Phil) mentors to a "manhood ceremony" to celebrate his eighteenth birthday, and christen him as a rite of passage. The drill was that we would eat together, share with him what it means to be a man, and then call out the positive virtues we see in his life. Each man stood and shared decades of hard-earned wisdom. It was a profound experience to see each of them speak life into my son. And then, it was my turn.

I could have told him to honor his future wife, to work hard, to leave a rich legacy, or a host of other virtues and values. However, one ideal stood above the rest. So I stood, thanked the gentlemen around the table, and then shared, "Son, the number one thing you must do as a man is to recognize divine relationships and cling to them."

That day, my son experienced the incredible power of input relationships, and I believe the wisdom he received changed his life. This is just a glimpse of what's to come for him if he continues to value relationships like these. And I believe the same is true for you. If you and I use wisdom and discernment in selecting these input, neutral, and output relationships, and stay engaged in the process of managing them, I fully believe that they will crown our lives with blessing.

SECTION 9:

RESOLUTIONS

NOW, I KNOW THAT WHEN we think of resolutions, we immediately think of firm commitments we make at the beginning of every year. For this section, we are not considering resolutions as "New Year's" resolutions. I liken this concept to one that I practiced while serving on a municipal board. At the end of every public meeting, our executive director would summarize the minutes, action items, and *resolutions* of the board. These were actions the board took that exercised authority, implemented policy, and spent or procured resources.

Simply put, they were what we were resolved as a body *to do* and *not to do.*

You can think of your resolutions as your personal code of conduct or standards of behavior. Each of the leaders we interviewed had a code of conduct, in many ways higher than the standards of the organizations they led. It's important to note that the way these people constructed their code of conduct involved a high degree of exposure, perspective, and accountability. For example, many of the people we studied had documented or nondocumented "rules of engagement" for how they interface with coworkers, vendors, and the general public. They ensured the compliance of these (and other) key resolutions by inviting multiple sets of eyes on themselves—which, in turn, produced the accountability and protection they desired.

For them, this practice provided a tremendous advantage in maintaining alignment with their core convictions and protecting themselves and their organizations. This level of clarity offered freedom to express their leadership within the guardrails of the safe, preset boundaries we call *resolutions*, and it can do the same for us as well.

For instance, when my children were little, I had way more peace and rest in my heart when they played in the backyard as opposed to the front yard. And the only difference between the two was a fence (a boundary).

If you're thinking of the different categories of resolutions, a good framework to start with is to look at how you currently live, and then craft resolutions in the big three: resources, people, and time. In this section, we will work through examples of each.

> **Resources:** personal and professional assets.
>
> **People:** communication (social media, email, text, etc.) and in-person connection (policies related to coworkers, clients, friends, and the public).

Time: calendar (where you spend your time, and your policies for travel, hotels, transportation, etc.).

Together, our goal is to do two things with each consideration:

1. Create your resolutions (what is the policy or code of conduct?)
2. Apply the *EPA Advantage* (who has eyes on this resolution?)

After seeing this in the lives of the people we studied, I went to work creating my own resolutions. Today, I have a clear policy for every category above, as well as multiple sets of eyes and accountability metrics for each. While I must confess that I am still a work in progress, make poor choices at times, and am sometimes tempted to compromise, I am in a much better position to live and lead because of these resolutions. In my observation, the primary reason these leaders formed this structure was to safeguard their platform from two potential enemies: the enemy within and the enemy without (i.e., themselves and others). Ultimately, it establishes an invisible identity, or character, in the visible leader that guides them and is known by those around them.

The great news for you is that you have full creative latitude on how you execute this. In the Marines that wasn't the case. We were issued a USMC code of conduct and were expected to comply one hundred percent with that code. If we transgressed that code, and it was reported, there was a potential for charges to be brought against us that could lead up to court martial under the Uniformed Code of Military Justice (UCMJ). The judgment could read, "Conduct unbecoming a United States Marine." The reason they issued this code is because we were expected to reflect positively upon the USMC, the U.S. Navy, and ultimately the United States of America.

Our encouragement for you to create your resolutions is possibly of higher consequence. Your legacy is at stake. In Section Two, *Design*, we'll guide you through the creation of your resolutions with practical examples.

RESOURCES: PERSONAL AND PROFESSIONAL ASSETS

Leaders who voluntarily place their financial stewardship habits (spending, giving, saving, investing) under scrutiny are simply less likely to experience compromise or misalignment with their values. If you have a clear policy for how you steward, *plus* multiple sets of eyes on your activities, it creates freedom—not prohibition. In short, I utilize the wisdom of a "financial team" to assist me in creating my resolutions, and certain parties of that team have limited, or full, access to all my activities, giving me the *EPA Advantage* I'm looking for.

As leaders, the more resources we steward, typically the more scrutiny we come under and the higher the stakes. You can learn a lot about someone's character by looking at how they steward finances. Creating your resolutions and applying the *EPA Advantage* to your finances will help you achieve the desired outcomes that are founded upon your values.

PEOPLE: COMMUNICATION AND IN-PERSON CONNECTION

Communication

Communication in our modern, technological world is easier—but more complex—than ever. Opportunities to interface with people are abundant. Our interactions are no longer limited to face-to-face meetings or phone calls. You can text, Facetime, Facebook message, Instagram, email, and on and on. Too much can be said, misinterpreted, or hidden if we're not careful and conscious of how we communicate.

As a leader, how have you committed to being transparent in the areas of your life where media is a tool? Who has access to your email, voicemail, phone, text messages, and social media accounts? Can you leave your phone on the coffee table without concern? Can you leave your laptop open without a second thought? If someone looked through your text messages, what would they see—would it align with your moral code?

In-Person Connection

Your level of responsibility dictates your level of accessibility. I understand the desire to communicate that you have an "open door" policy, and that you want to be available to your team at all times. However, if you make yourself accessible to everyone all of the time, you run the risk of becoming inefficient, unproductive,

“

YOUR LEVEL OF RESPONSIBILITY DICTATES YOUR LEVEL OF ACCESSIBILITY.”

unfocused, and vulnerable. I have routinely worked with clients who run multimillion-dollar businesses, and as their success grows, their systems, procedures, and accessibility adjusts a bit. They are responsible for more people, and the stakes are higher. And in addition to that, how they interact with people sets the tone for the entire organization or business they lead.

Adjusting how and when you interact with people doesn't mean closing yourself off to growth opportunities or healthy relationships that could challenge or encourage you. Discernment is the key. Many top-level leaders have an "open-door" policy, but try stopping by unannounced or popping in to say hello. You'll run smack-dab into a gatekeeper—their executive assistant, chief of staff, or scheduler. That extra layer around leadership doesn't make them bad leaders; it often makes them highly efficient. And it holds them accountable for how they interface with people.

When I requested to interview a sitting commanding general, I had to do so through his assistant, then staff attorney, then chief of staff. I was then asked to send questions ahead of time, and when I got to the location, I was led through several layers of people before finally sitting down and seeing the whites of his eyes. It's smart. It's necessary.

We now live in a society that requires us to have standards for how we interact with others—no matter who it is. What is your policy on meeting, texting, and communicating one-on-one with others?

TIME: CALENDAR AND TRAVEL

Calendar

Based on what I observed, I encourage a process where multiple people know who you're meeting with at any time. My calendar is exposed to my assistant, my team, and my spouse. Our personal calendar is actually synced with my professional calendar. This helps in multiple ways:

1. Planning: our personal/professional calendars rarely overlap.
2. Interruptions: because we have mutual vantage, we rarely interrupt business meetings or calls.
3. Confidence: we each know where the other is throughout the day.

In creating your calendar resolutions, you can apply the *EPA Advantage* to ensure that your code of conduct and moral code are aligned. Whether it's sharing your calendar with multiple team members … a policy for traveling alone or with someone else … a GPS tracker app on your phone in case of emergencies … you have to decide what fits your level of comfort and stewardship.

Travel

While we recognize that not everyone carries the weight of scrutiny, we thought it would be interesting to illustrate a travel resolution in the life of Billy Graham. When Reverend Graham was active in the ministry, the Charlotte-born evangelist held tight to the moral code that long-governed his life and leadership. At the height of his career, Graham's security team did a sweep of his hotel room each night, making sure no one else was in the room. The "Billy Graham rule" has since been used by many leaders around the world who have dialed into resolutions that reflect their desired character.[18] Graham, whose life was never tainted by scandal, knew something we could all benefit from—living a life above reproach is always worth it.

Just to be clear, none of the leaders that we interviewed had policies as severe as "The Billy Graham rule." However, for the most part, all of the leaders we interviewed had a clear policy for their calendar and travel, including multiple sets of eyes for accountability.

CONCLUDING THOUGHTS ON RESOLUTIONS

Even as I'm writing this, I'm aware that this could feel somewhat restrictive in nature. But remember who I'm writing this to. You, a leader. And remember, the greater your influence, the greater the consequences if you compromise your moral or ethical code. This is a fact I'm acutely aware of.

My clients come to me for vision, winning strategies, and increased performance. They come for growth in business *and* in life.

---

[18] https://www.thegospelcoalition.org/blogs/evangelical-history/where-did-the-billy-graham-rule-come-from/

They want relational harmony in the home and in the office—and they need healthy life rhythms to hold it all together. And while I've made a career out of helping them achieve these things, I've also concluded that you cannot give away what you don't have.

For me, setting and *keeping* my resolutions isn't a nice ideal, it's a necessary one. I'm certainly not a golden boy, and I'm far from perfect. But I know that for me to break my personal and professional resolutions puts me at incredible risk. As I write this, my consulting business has a national platform. I'm a husband of twenty-three years and have five children. Like you, I've worked incredibly hard for the life I have. And resolutions are like the guardrails that keep my vehicle from tumbling off a cliff.

While nobody has the whole package, anyone with a leadership platform must be aware of the stakes. As leaders, we are held to a higher standard. And once you put on the leadership hat, you put yourself under scrutiny. Why? Because you're influencing others.

For me, resolutions have provided concrete standards to live up to, rather than whims that change based on how I'm feeling. The same is true for my clients and can be for you as well. Honestly, I've never regretted higher standards—and have yet to meet anyone who has. But I've always regretted lower ones. Creating standards and opening ourselves to healthy relationships are key ingredients in the recipe for successful living.

So what about you? How do you start? One step at a time. How do you sustain it? It's all about rhythms, which is what we are talking about next.

SECTION 10:

RHYTHMS

★ ★ ★

LEADERSHIP IS BOTH FULFILLING and rewarding. However, at times, it can truly come at a price. In my observation, second to vision, the most attractive element of a leader is their energy level. The reason leaders can move people from point A to point B is because of the sheer force of their magnetic energy that draws people into a picture of a preferable future. In this section of the book, we will be describing the three primary chambers of a leader's "battery cell" and how to monitor and sustain a high energy level.

Before we describe these chambers and how you can apply a plan, along with the *EPA advantage*, to produce sustainable energy in your life and leadership, I want to tell you why I believe rhythms are so important. Two of the leaders we studied experienced tremendous loss because they compromised their moral code. In both cases, this loss affected the entire nation, the states where they held seats of authority, and most certainly, their family members. In the post-trauma investigation of *why* their compromise occurred, both declared the same conclusion: they consistently found themselves in a depleted state, and their compromise was an attempt to serve a legitimate need, illegitimately.

I want to draw your attention to one more powerful conclusion. Both of these leaders had their relationships intact and their resolutions set, but their rhythms (self-care) were so neglected that when the choice to compromise presented itself, they lacked the energy, strength, and presence of mind to maintain the level of integrity consistent with their character. Both of these individuals carried global and national influence, and the demands of their offices were great. However, what led to the compromise was truly their inability to say no to the demands of others at the expense of their own quality of life. So you see, this is an excellent example of leaders doing something good for others, but experiencing a traumatic and awful result for themselves. In this section, I hope to convince you to prioritize yourself by monitoring your energy level. Unless you can breathe, it's difficult to provide oxygen for those you are leading.

Your rhythms replenish all three chambers of your battery cell: spirit & soul, physical & medical, and mental & emotional. Simply put, if the chambers are full, they add energy to you. If the chambers are empty, they rob you of it. This matters because consistently living in a depleted state can become a breeding ground for compromise. In our research, we found that those who sustained their leadership seat with little or no moral, ethical, or financial compromise endured through rhythms of rest and recharging. They balanced the spiritual, emotional, mental, and physical loads of high-stress careers by operating from an internal place of wholeness.

Greg Salciccioli captures this best in his book, *The Enemies of Excellence: 7 Reasons Why We Sabotage Success*. In the book, Coach Greg describes a concept called "systematic renewal," which is an attempt to preemptively and consistently apply the discipline of charging your life's battery. Essentially, the concept declares that if human beings add energy to themselves when they don't need it, the battery will be full when they do need it. Coach Greg goes on to describe practical methods to apply this to your life. While systematic renewal takes a high degree of discipline and intentionality, in my opinion, it is one of the strongest safeguards for healthy living and leading.

In Part Two, the design portion of this book, you will develop your unique rhythms more clearly. However, to establish mindshare, we want to briefly introduce the chambers to you now.

SPIRIT & SOUL

This is the dimension of who you are at your core. To use a bad metaphor from the Marines, it is your central command post, the place you are receiving purpose, guidance, wisdom, comfort, joy, peace, and all of the intangible elements that make up the human experience (see my *5Gs Journal* for guidance).[19]

---

[19] Available in digital and print forms at LegendaryLeadershipConsultants.com.

The demands of leadership are great. Every leader I know has the propensity to fire off their day as soon as their eyes open and feet hit the ground. The best leaders I know, however, have learned the discipline of quieting their soul and filling their hearts with the inspiration necessary to serve the world around them. Our spirits can be nourished or starved. When I meet with God in the morning, I start my day with a rested soul, an alert mind, and a full heart. This empowers me to walk slowly through the crowd, and lead with the focus, intentionality, and energy needed to accomplish my mission for the day.

PHYSICAL & MEDICAL

The second area is your physical well-being. I don't have to be a doctor to tell you that stress creates a lot of wear and tear on the body. People under stress can suffer an incredible number of health problems, including insomnia, weight gain, high blood pressure, and on and on. Your body is one of the most keen indicators to your mental and emotional health. In this category, you're not measuring only your waist size, body mass index, or weight. It also includes your holistic medical health.

MENTAL & EMOTIONAL

The third area to monitor is your mental state—or mindset. These are our beliefs rooted either in "abundance" or "scarcity." An abundance mindset sees unlimited potential, even in the most difficult circumstances. Abundant leaders believe incredible success isn't simply possible but inevitable! To the contrary, a scarcity mindset focuses on obstacles over opportunities. Rather than limitless growth, this mindset sees scarce potential. Simply put, in a scarcity mindset, there isn't enough to go around.

How you deal with your thought life, or what leading psychologists call your "self-talk," is extremely important for people who make decisions or create policy on a daily basis. An abundance mindset and healthy self-talk creates mental resilience and powers growth, even through mistakes and adverse circumstances beyond our control. The mental game is where the battle is won or lost—and keeping this battery cell at full charge is the first step of winning that battle.

Our emotional state is another invisible dimension of a person, consisting of their "feeling" life. It is tightly connected with our mental lives, and both certainly can rob or fill a person with energy. These are emotional states such as happiness or sadness, pain or pleasure, ecstasy or anxiety, fear or faith, panic or peace, and more.

Think of our emotional states like our smartphones. If we leave a bunch of applications open in the background, the symptom we would experience is rapid depletion of our cell phone battery. The root cause of that symptom would be unattended (and unresolved) "app windows" that are utilizing precious emotional energy.

Many leaders we studied cited personal issues that created a steady drag on their emotions, which certainly affected their professional life. Just as the physical and emotional realms are connected, the personal and professional are as well. However you analyze it, we can all agree that a neglected emotional state can result in little to no margin or bandwidth to be your best.

CONCLUDING THOUGHTS ON RHYTHMS

The higher we rise in our leadership and influence, the more responsibilities and rewards, opportunities and challenges, distractions and achievements we will experience. We can have solid relationships intact, and clear resolutions, but if we attempt to serve from a depleted state, we run a high risk of experiencing compromise and regret. That being said, you may be reading this now and saying, "Phil, that's me. I'm on 'E.' What can I do about it now?"

A number of years ago I started working with a young leader who also found himself running on empty. On the outside, everything looked great. His company was growing and landing large contracts. He had a beautiful family and seemed to be happily married. He's the kind of guy who had it all—and at an early age. However, while his star appeared to be rising, things weren't as they seemed.

A couple of these large contracts came with unanticipated consequences, which is what led him to me. In a strategic planning session, he laid out what was really going on behind the scenes. Some of his international clients were holding money ransom, pushing off invoices, and making him carry the financial burden of the business relationship. In short, this "corporate bullying" produced tremendous stress on him and his team. And even after consistent legal action, they couldn't gain back the ground they'd lost.

The professional stress caused him to focus all of his energy on solving the pain points of the business, and over time, neglect many of the healthy rhythms that made him successful in the first place. Unhealthy habits and coping mechanisms formed, healthy rhythms faded, and compromise became common. Before he knew it, he had spun into a dark place where he felt like the walls were caving in and he couldn't breathe. Many times he would come into our session and we wouldn't talk for the first fifteen minutes. It was all he could do to drag himself to session with the tremendous pain he was carrying in both his personal and professional lives.

Back at home, the arguments grew more intense and a lack of fulfillment consistently haunted him. He started to believe his "self-talk" that he hadn't just experienced degrees of failure—but that he himself was a failure.

My heart went out to him as he explained the reality of his situation. Together, we developed a vision for what he wanted to accomplish in his business *and* personal life. Despite his best efforts, unfortunately, he experienced loss in both areas. It seemed to both of us that we started working together a bit too late. The loss he experienced in his professional and personal life was extremely painful for both of us. However, his story didn't stop there.

What seemed like a *fatal setback* actually became a *fortunate setup*. Together, we worked our way through the three layers of his life—public, private, and secret—and devised strategies to align them with his personal moral code. Step by step, he began living a fully-integrated life. By inviting exposure, perspective, and accountability (the *EPA Advantage*) in his relationships, resolutions, and rhythms, he laid a sturdy foundation.

I'm happy to report that today, because of these systems, he's flourishing. He enjoys a healthy family life, and is one of the most successful people in his field. Best of all, as I write these words, he is enjoying the fruit of his effort in peace, prosperity, confidence, and stability. He's living by design instead of default. And his intentionality in key relationships, resolutions, and rhythms protects him from repeating the compromise that cost him so dearly.

His story makes me smile because it's a reminder that we're never too far down the path to move our lives in a more positive direction. Whether you're a young person and the game is just beginning… Or you're somewhere near halftime, like me… Or even in your fourth quarter… It's never too late to live by design instead of default.

GOOD SUCCESS

The more I live, the more I'm convinced that there are two kinds of success: good success and bad success. Bad success comes through bad character and compromise; a pursuit of pleasure, prosperity, or gain at the expense of your core convictions and those of others. Bad success creates two losers: others externally and you internally. As my client learned, the "corporate bully" that inflicted so much pain may have turned a profit that year when the dust settled, but they left a wake of death and destruction behind them. They may have looked good on the outside, but their reputation is tarnished forever.

Good success, on the other hand, comes through sterling character. In contrast to bad success, it produces two winners: others externally and you internally. Knowing you've conducted your business well produces a deep sense of satisfaction. Good success can be found in the way you treat your employees and vendors, the way you approach legal matters, the fairness with which you conduct your business, and the graciousness with which you approach relationships. It means alignment with your core convictions. It means integrity that results in authentic, confident, and fearless leadership. Good success creates peace, fulfillment, and joy. And it is the aim of the second portion of this book.

Now, let's get to work designing your *good* success.

PART TWO:

DESIGN

I BELIEVE THE HEALTH of our society is directly related to the health of its leaders. In Part Two, you will create your personal *Character Code*, inviting health and sustainability into every area of your life.

How you approach this part of the book is important. Find a quiet, peaceful place where you can reflect and unplug as much as possible. Turn off your cell phone and give yourself some buffer to give this the time it needs. Also, remember, this is your *Character Code* and no one is going to read this but you.

We have divided your work into three exercises related to how you steward **relationships**, maintain your personal and professional **resolutions**, and recharge your battery cells through healthy **rhythms**.

This portion of the book can power a massive advantage in your life and leadership. But that power is greatly abated if action items are not documented, and execution is mismanaged. Because of this, we created **Action Item Summary Pages**, as well as a community of high-caliber leaders like you to provide accountability. Visit OurSecretLifeBook.com to learn more.

The end goal of these exercises is to summarize the action steps you need to take to improve the health of your relationships, resolutions, and rhythms. You will populate the Action Item Summary Pages (starting on page 154) with action items that need to be delegated or completed by you.

You can use the exercise templates in this book or visit OurSecretLifeBook.com to download a printable *Character Code* workbook.

RELATIONSHIPS

★ ★ ★

AS LEADERS, WE ARE stronger and more enduring when we invest in, and avail ourselves to, relationships. In this exercise, you will outline your relationships in three areas: input, neutral, and output. Some of us have an abundance of relationships, while some of us have very few. The important principle to embrace when creating your relationship spoke wheel is to have balance in all three relational areas—commensurate with the season of life you are in.

Let's define each area and then move on to the exercise.

I. **Input Relationships** are those that provide you with wise counsel professionally, spiritually, financially, relationally, personally, etc. These may be organic or contractual.

II. **Neutral Relationships** are friendships where you can "turn off." You don't have to be the leader. Instead, you can enjoy the wonderful fellowship of a good friend.

III. Output Relationships are those where you are investing in a person to help them maximize their potential. You might be coaching, mentoring, or teaching them in a one-on-one or group setting.

In the next pages, you will find three sections:

- our guided sample exercises,
- your working exercises,
- and your action plan.

Also included are questions to provoke thoughts about existing and potential relationships. The sample relational health assessment shows what these areas might look like, how they fit together, and your current assessment of each.

Please review the samples and then continue through the exercise to complete your own.

SAMPLE: RELATIONAL HEALTH ASSESSMENT

You will find three tables, one for each relational area. The purpose of the tables is to help you see the current depth of each area and assess its health on a 1–10 scale (10 being healthy, and 1 being unhealthy).

Use these values to obtain your overall health scores:

- 10 (Healthy) = Energizing (open, honest, mutual respect)
- 1 (Unhealthy) = Draining (burned out, dishonest, nonreciprocal)

Next, write an action step for "What needs to change?" for growth to occur.

Helpful guides for these action steps are:

- **Frequency of connection.** Do you need more or less time together? How regular is the cadence?
- **Desired outcome.** Do you have a clear, desired outcome for this connectivity? What do you hope to achieve in your time together?
- **Mutual value.** What value are they adding to you—and what value are you adding to them? Do you have common interests and hobbies?
- **Agenda.** For your *input* and *output* relationships, do you honor time (yours and theirs) with a clear agenda? Intentionality with time creates desired outcomes.

- **Turning off.** For your neutral relationships, are you able to "turn off" and just be yourself? Can you step off the stage of leadership and into the ease of friendship?

Once the grid is filled in, the row at the bottom of each table offers a space to add a subtotal and divide into the average health of the total area. This simple metric affords a helpful vantage to gauge where you are today.

You may have more (or fewer) relationships in each area than the rows provided. That's okay! In fact, if you find you're a little light in any relational area, use this as an opportunity to list the names of people you'd like to forge new relationships with.

For my samples, I'm going to list the types of relationships someone might have—rather than specific names. Allow these categories to act as a guide to spark ideas.

Consider my example for input relationships.

JOHN DOE NAME			
INPUT RELATIONSHIPS	ASSESS (1–10)	WHAT NEEDS TO CHANGE?	
SPIRITUAL	7	Meet monthly w/Pastor Danny on growth plan	
COUNSELOR	5	Schedule time & frequency w/Don Joe, LPC	
MENTOR	7	Create meeting agenda with Mr. Bob	
COACH	8	Outline goals for session with Brandon	
PROFESSIONAL SERVICES	6	Schedule meetings with CPA and attorney	
SUBTOTAL	33	INPUT RELATIONSHIPS HEALTH	6.6

Once completed, I add the sum of each relationship's current assessment, placing that sum into the subtotal. Then, I calculate the overall average score for input relationship health by dividing the subtotal by the number of relationships listed.

In my example above, I listed five relationships, with a subtotal assessment of 33. Then I divided the subtotal (33) by 5, to get an average health score of 6.6 out of 10. Now I have a benchmark and action steps to grow each relationship!

Next, I will complete neutral and output relationship tables and calculate my total relational health.

NEUTRAL RELATIONSHIPS	ASSESS (1-10)	WHAT NEEDS TO CHANGE?	
FRIENDS	4	Schedule lunch to plan guys' trip	
COUSIN	6	Setup Zoom to discuss reunion	
BROTHERS	7	Plan holiday parties for the year	
CIGAR BUDDY	5	Setup cigar night for next week	
FISHING BUDDY	4	Reserve weekend at the camp	
SUBTOTAL	26	NEUTRAL RELATIONSHIPS HEALTH	5.2

OUTPUT RELATIONSHIPS	ASSESS (1-10)	WHAT NEEDS TO CHANGE?	
CHILDREN	4	Plan group + individual connect time	
BUSINESS MENTEE	6	Guide Daniel through life plan	
SPIRITUAL MENTEE	7	Meet for coffee weekly on Thursdays	
MEN'S GROUP	5	Set dates to lead 12 week study	
SUBTOTAL	22	OUTPUT RELATIONSHIPS HEALTH	5.5

I have now completed each relational area and calculated the average health for each. It's now time to sum up my overall relational health score.

To do so, I add the average health scores from each area into the corresponding boxes, then add them together, writing the total in the sum box. Next, I divide by 3 to find my overall relational health score.

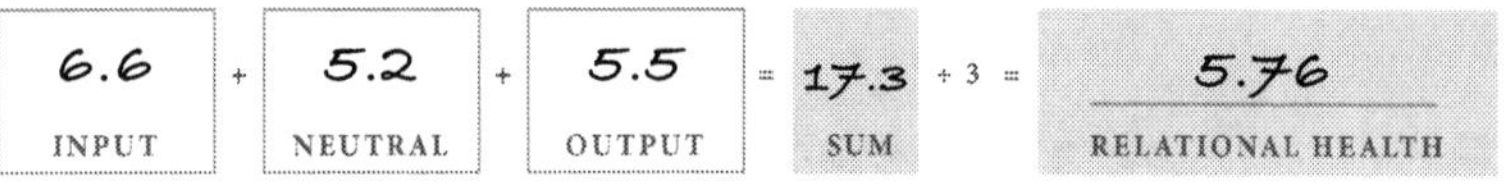

QUESTIONS TO CONSIDER

Now it's your turn to complete your relational assessment and relational tree! To help you on your way, I've included some questions to consider as you cultivate the relationships that will invite greater perspective and health into your life.

INPUT:

- Who are your spiritual voices?
- Who are your strategic voices?
- Who are your professional voices?

NEUTRAL:

- Who can you "turn off" around?
- Who do you share common interests with?
- Who do you share common values with?

OUTPUT:

- Who do you invest in?
- Who would best steward your investment in them for maximum return?
- Who would you like to help grow?

YOUR RELATIONAL HEALTH ASSESSMENT

NAME ______________________

INPUT RELATIONSHIPS	ASSESS (1-10)	WHAT NEEDS TO CHANGE?	
SUBTOTAL		INPUT RELATIONSHIPS HEALTH	

NEUTRAL RELATIONSHIPS	ASSESS (1-10)	WHAT NEEDS TO CHANGE?	
SUBTOTAL		NEUTRAL RELATIONSHIPS HEALTH	

OUTPUT RELATIONSHIPS	ASSESS (1-10)	WHAT NEEDS TO CHANGE?	
SUBTOTAL		OUTPUT RELATIONSHIPS HEALTH	

INPUT + NEUTRAL + OUTPUT = SUM ÷ 3 = RELATIONAL HEALTH

SAMPLE: RELATIONAL TREE

Now that I've shown John Doe's input, neutral, and output relationships defined, assessed, and with a charted course for growth, I will map them onto a relational tree. Just like the mighty oak trees that are better together, seeing relationships as a unified whole is both rewarding and illuminating.

I will begin by writing John's name at the center and then fill in the names of the meaningful relationships branching throughout his life. I have also jotted down the category of each relationship for clarity, and an overall view of what kind of relationships he has today—and what new relationships he may like to seek out.

To complete your own relational tree, you will simply fill in the names you just identified in your relational health assessment tables.

Here is a snapshot of our relational tree to guide you.

EXAMPLE: RELATIONAL TREE

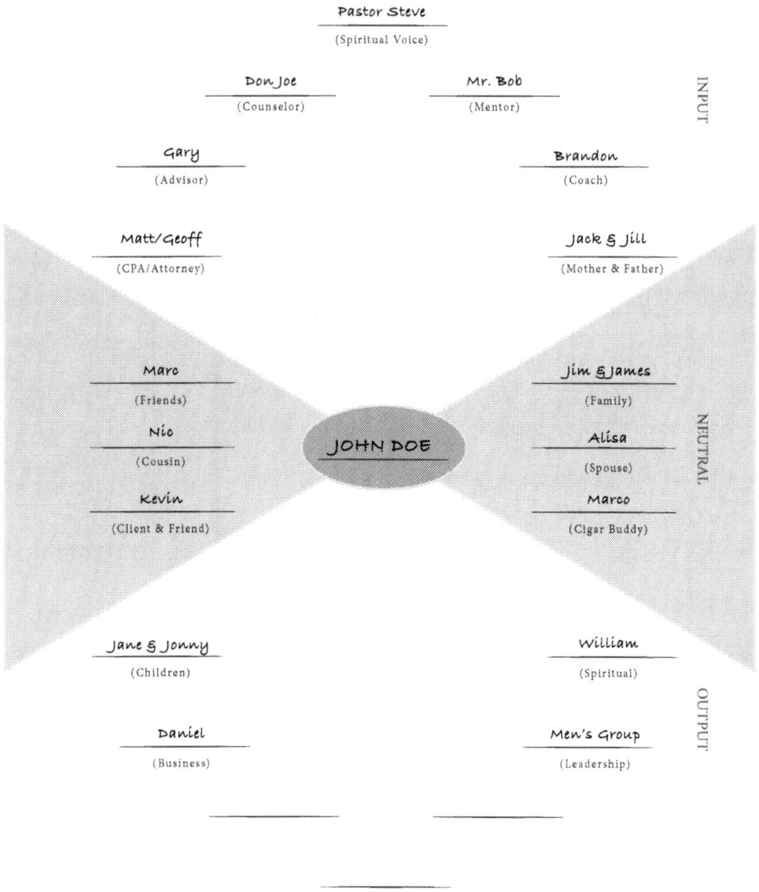

YOUR RELATIONAL TREE

RELATIONAL TREE

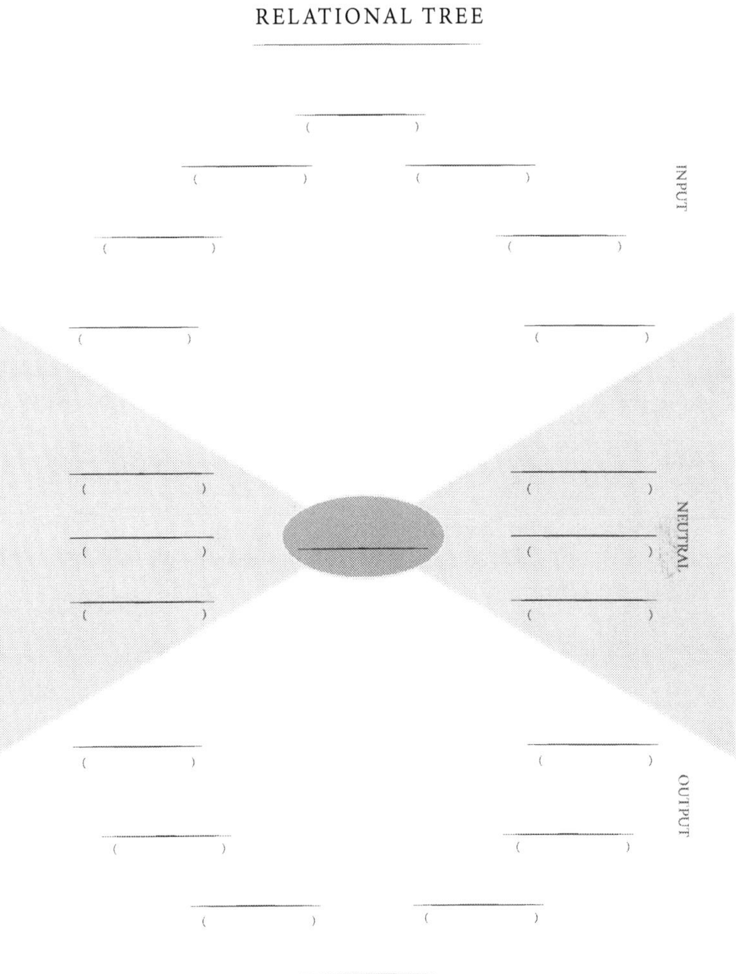

TAKE ACTION

Congratulations on taking this step toward building healthy relationships!

While names may change over the course of time, you now have an enduring pattern to monitor your relational health.

Now it's time to take what you've learned from your relational health assessment and write down the action steps you need to take to optimize your relational health. Go to the Action Item Summary Page (on page 154) and fill in the action items that need to be completed by you or delegated to others.

Now let's turn to your **resolutions** as a leader.

RESOLUTIONS

★ ★ ★

IN THIS EXERCISE, YOU will craft your resolutions. Personally and professionally, what are you resolved *to do* and *not to do*? Your resolutions are your personal code of conduct and/or standards of behavior. Remember, the leaders who we studied maintained high standards for themselves—many times higher than the organizations they led. Consider stretching when developing your resolutions.

The key to maintaining your resolutions is employing the *EPA Advantage*—or giving yourself the advantage of a high degree of exposure, perspective, and accountability. This practice helps maintain tremendous alignment with your desired outcomes.

In the next pages, you will find three sections:

- our guided sample exercises,
- your working exercises,
- and your action plan.

We have divided them into three categories:

1. **Resources** (personal and professional finances/assets)
2. **People** (communication and in-person connection)
3. **Time** (calendar and travel)

SAMPLE: RESOURCES

Let's walk through a sample showing how to create a leader's unique code of conduct for their personal and professional resources. To start, we will outline her *EPA Advantage* team, using fictitious examples from a leader's personal and professional life.

The question to answer is this: whose eyes are on every dollar that comes in and every dollar that goes out? These are the people who have appropriate visibility into how she handles her finances—from large expenses to petty cash.

This leader has six sets of eyes on her finances to employ the *EPA Advantage*.

($) RESOURCES

EPA ADVANTAGE TEAM

CPA	Financial Advisor
Director of Finance	Business Partner
Spouse	Bookkeeper

This team gives her an amazing advantage, a lifted perspective, *and* accountability to keep her stewardship aligned with her code of conduct. This code forms the basis of her written resolutions, or what she *will do* and *won't do.*

In Resources, it was critical for this leader to separate her personal and professional funds and allow no intermingling.

So, we will consider her finances in the following four categories, both personally and professionally:

1. **Spend:** What money goes out each month? Debt?
2. **Save:** What money stays in the bank account each month?
3. **Invest:** What funds will she put to work each month?
4. **Give:** How will she practice generosity each month?

Next, let's review the samples for her resources and code of conduct to guide you in your own exercise.

RESOURCES

EPA ADVANTAGE TEAM

CPA	Financial Advisor
Director of Finance	Business Partner
Spouse	Bookkeeper

CODE OF CONDUCT

	PERSONAL POLICY	PROFESSIONAL POLICY
SPEND	• 70% of total income on taxes and person budget	• Keep payroll and operating expenses to 55% of total budget
SAVE	• The first 5% of total income paid into savings account	• 30% EBITDA • Save 5% for working capital
INVEST	• 5% of income into Roth IRAs, stock market, and real estate holdings • 5% of income toward add'l debt repayment (properties, etc.)	• Invest 2.5% of revenue into research & development or innovation • Invest 2.5% for employee professional development
GIVE	• 15% of total income to selected charities and church	• Give 100 probono hours per year to worthy causes • Host fundraising dinner for selected nonprofits • Sponsor tournaments, Little League teams, etc.

After outlining her plan with the resources she stewards, let's look at her plans for:

1. How she connects with **people** via communication and in-person connection
2. How she manages her **time** through her calendar and travel policy

PEOPLE

EPA ADVANTAGE TEAM

Executive Assistant	Marketing Manager
Spouse	

CODE OF CONDUCT

	PERSONAL POLICY	PROFESSIONAL POLICY
COMMUNICATION	• Although I control my personal social media and email accounts, my professional team will still have access because my personal life impacts my professional life • I conduct my personal communication (text, phone, email, social media) in such a way that at any moment one of my kids or grandkids could pick up my phone without me worrying about it • I only password protect confidential material that honors and protects my constituents	• My email and social media will be accessible (and managed) by my executive assistant and—when applica-ple—my marketing manager • My team will sign nondisclosure agreements when applicable • My outward communication will always represent our core values
IN-PERSON CONNECTION	• Will come across as hospitable, warm, and friendly • My person is always accounted for (e.g. Life360 application, find my phone app, calendar, etc.)	• Will do everything in my power to project the tenants of my faith and good will toward others • 1-on-1 meetings will occur behind open-door/glass windows when possible • Meetings (other than staff) must be scheduled through assistant or team • [General rule] Clear agenda for purpose of every meeting

TIME

EPA ADVANTAGE TEAM

Executive Assistant	Chief of Staff
Spouse	

CODE OF CONDUCT

	PERSONAL POLICY	PROFESSIONAL POLICY
CALENDAR	• Accessible by my EPA Advantage team • Calendar created in Q4 for the year ahead • Personal calendar is color-coded and overlayed into professional to avoid scheduling conflicts • Weekly (Sunday evening) look-ahead discussion with spouse	• Will share with my EPA Advantage team • Calendar created in Q4 for the year ahead • I time-block priorities and disciplines (unrelated to work) to include special projects that explore future opportunities
TRAVEL	• Anybody I travel with, I explain squarely my convictions, only traveling with those who can respect them	• I will travel less than 25% of working time • I will have itineraries available to my team • When possible, I travel with a team member or associate • If I fly first class, my employees and associates will as well

As you turn the pages to create your codes of conduct, there are key considerations for each area: resources (personal and professional finances), people (communication and in-person connection), and time (calendar and travel).

QUESTIONS TO CONSIDER

RESOURCES (personal and professional finances):

- Who is your *EPA Advantage* team?
- Is there any aspect of your personal or professional finances that does not have multiple sets of eyes on it?
- Are your current practices aligned with your desired code of conduct?

PEOPLE (communication and in-person connection):

- Who is your *EPA Advantage* team?
- What channels of communication do you use most frequently?
- Are there proper layers between yourself and others to guard access to your person (or media)?
- Do you want/need/have a code of conduct for private meetings, to protect you and others?

TIME (calendar and travel):

- Who is your *EPA Advantage* team?
- Is your personal location accounted for at all times?
- Do you have a personal travel policy? (e.g., do you travel alone? How often do you travel? [load versus capacity] etc.)

YOUR CODES OF CONDUCT

Now it's your turn to craft your plan (a framework that informs your code of conduct). Please take time to carefully consider each area and its impact on your life, leadership, and legacy. Use this opportunity to double down in the areas of your life where your code of conduct is strong—and firm it up where there are potential weaknesses.

You will find three exercises in sequence:

1. Resources (personal and professional)
2. People (communication and in-person connection)
3. Time (calendar and travel)

After working through each area, you will find a final section to summarize your resolutions statement and then outline your action steps for growth.

($) RESOURCES EPA ADVANTAGE TEAM

PLAN: FRAMEWORK THAT INFORMS CODE OF CONDUCT

	PERSONAL POLICY	PROFESSIONAL POLICY
SPEND		
SAVE		
INVEST		
GIVE		

PEOPLE

EPA ADVANTAGE TEAM

PLAN: FRAMEWORK THAT INFORMS CODE OF CONDUCT

	PERSONAL POLICY	PROFESSIONAL POLICY
COMMUNICATION		
IN-PERSON CONNECTION		

TIME

EPA ADVANTAGE TEAM

PLAN: FRAMEWORK THAT INFORMS CODE OF CONDUCT

	PERSONAL POLICY	PROFESSIONAL POLICY
CALENDAR		
TRAVEL		

SAMPLE: RESOLUTIONS STATEMENT

A resolution statement is a powerful thing because our words carry weight. Living in alignment with our resolutions can create predictable patterns that establish our character. And ultimately, protect us from compromise and accusation. It ensures our life and leadership are above reproach with the *EPA Advantage* applied to each.

Here is an example of what a completed ***resolutions statement*** *might look like.*

RESOLUTIONS STATEMENT

I, SAMPLE LEADER, am resolved to apply the EPA Advantage in my personal and professional life. I will invite exposure, perspective, and accountability into the stewardship of all of my RESOURCES, PEOPLE, and TIME.

I will be completely accountable to my team in the following Code of Conduct.

WITH MY RESOURCES, I RESOLVE TO invest more than I spend, be a good steward of the resources entrusted to me, and contribute more than I consume.

AND I RESOLVE NOT TO invest in people or companies that don't reflect my values, or anything that violates my personal moral code.

WITH PEOPLE, I RESOLVE TO conduct all communication in a way that honors both personal and professional relationships and open both my calendar and location to my EPA Team.

AND I RESOLVE NOT TO put myself, or anyone else, in a position with even the appearance of impropriety.

WITH MY TIME, I RESOLVE TO plan personal and professional calendar 6 mos. to 1 year in advance and time-block all priorities and key disciplines.

AND I RESOLVE NOT TO travel more than 25% of working time or travel alone when avoidable.

RESOLUTIONS STATEMENT

I, ______________________, am resolved to apply the EPA Advantage in my personal and professional life. I will invite exposure, perspective, and accountability into the stewardship of all of my RESOURCES, PEOPLE, and TIME.

I will be completely accountable to my team in the following Code of Conduct.

WITH MY RESOURCES, I RESOLVE TO ______________________

____

____

AND I RESOLVE NOT TO ______________________

____

____

WITH PEOPLE, I RESOLVE TO ______________________

____

____

AND I RESOLVE NOT TO ______________________

____

____

WITH MY TIME, I RESOLVE TO ______________________

____

____

AND I RESOLVE NOT TO ______________________

____

____

TAKE ACTION

While resolutions might seem restrictive in nature, our research reveals that they give leaders a larger perception of freedom to steward within the preset boundaries of their values. The greater your influence as a leader, the greater your opportunity for compromise *or* accusation, and ultimately, the greater the consequences for yourself and society. By defining your personal and professional codes of conduct in these critical areas, you set yourself up to enjoy an enduring legacy without moral, ethical, or financial failure.

So, I challenge you one last time: have you set resolutions that make you rise to a higher standard than those you lead?

Through personal experience and research, I have observed that leaders never regret high standards—but nearly always regret low ones.

Finally, share these resolutions with your *EPA Advantage* team, and ensure they have the access they need to help you keep them. Revisit these resolutions often, rise to the standards you have set for yourself, and enjoy the authenticity, confidence, and fearlessness this way of life and leadership provides.

Lastly, let's turn to your **rhythms**.

RHYTHMS

★ ★ ★

AS A LEADER, HOW is your energy level? Are you brimming with motivation and grit, or limping through endless cycles of burnout and fatigue? While leadership is fulfilling and rewarding, it *can* come with great personal cost to the leader and their family.

In the following exercises, you will build a supercharger for your energy to guarantee you never run on empty. You will lead with a full tank by observing healthy rhythms in three areas:

1. Spirit & Soul
2. Physical & Medical
3. Mental & Emotional

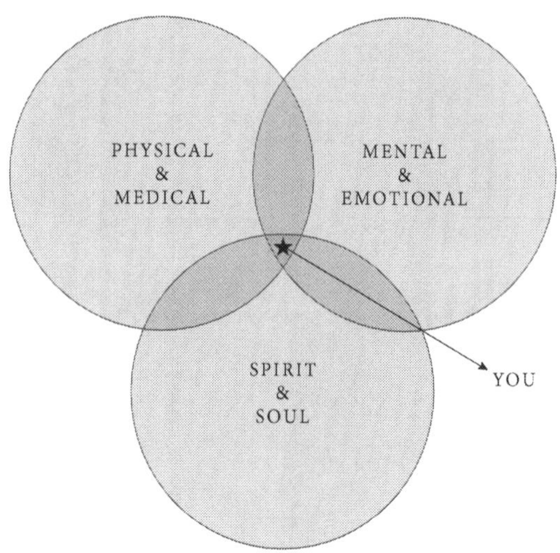

These three components can be viewed as the chambers of an individual's battery cell. When attended to, they will sustain you in every season of life and leadership. When neglected or mismanaged, however, massive fatigue can set in. We have found "energy depletion" to be the *largest threat* related to compromise.

In the next pages, you will find three sections:

- Our guided sample exercises
- Your working exercises
- Your action plan

The exercises will cover the three chambers of your battery cell and allow you to create the contributing factors to fullness, assess each area, and outline actions for growth.

Please review the examples and then continue through the exercise to complete your own.

EXAMPLE: SPIRIT & SOUL RHYTHMS BATTERY CELL

Each battery cell is arranged in five components: area, assessment, actions to grow, and overall health. Together, we will walk through the sample spirit and soul battery cell, analyzing rhythms and energy levels.

Assessments

You will begin by rating your overall health in this area. Then, the assessments consider the contributing factors that give you energy when regularly practiced, or drain your energy when neglected. For the spirit and soul aspect of our lives, we've outlined some of these practices below.

Whether yours are similar—or differ greatly—what's important is to find those recharging activities to keep you energized.

Then, after you have listed these contributing factors, assess their health on a scale of 1–10 (1 being poor, 10 being optimal). While your rating will be personal, let's consider things like the frequency and quality of each factor.

RATE THE OVERALL HEALTH OF YOUR SPIRIT & SOUL ON A 1-10 SCALE: 5

SPIRIT & SOUL

CONTRIBUTING FACTORS	ASSESSMENTS	1-10	ACTIONS TO GROW
	Devotions	4	✓
	Prayer	7	✓
	Worship	7	✓
	Church attendance	8	✓
	Small group	6	✓
	Family prayer	6	✓
	SUBTOTAL (Sum of all contributing factor ratings)		TOTAL ASSESSMENT (Sub-total divided by number of contributing factors)

Next, we will move on to the Actions to Grow column.

I have found that no matter how well I'm doing in a certain area, there is always room for improvement. And when an area is weak, it's an opportunity for me to make a substantial increase to my energy level by focusing on it.

So, we will write growth steps for each contributing factor on the matching line in the **Actions to Grow column**.

These are most effective when they are specific and actionable.

RATE THE OVERALL HEALTH OF YOUR SPIRIT & SOUL ON A 1-10 SCALE: 5

SPIRIT & SOUL			
ASSESSMENTS	1-10	ACTIONS TO GROW	
Devotions	4	Find new online devo (YouVersion)	
Prayer	7	Consistent time; 6am; home office	
Worship	7	Consistent time; 6:30am; home office	
Church attendance	8	Weekly with family	
Small group	6	Block off time and recommit	
Family prayer	6	If out of town call in	
SUBTOTAL (Sum of all contributing factor ratings)		TOTAL ASSESSMENT (Sub-total divided by number of contributing factors)	

CONTRIBUTING FACTORS

Finally, we will grade this battery cell, aiming for as close to a 100-percent charge as we can get—which would be a 10/10 rating. To calculate this, simply add the ratings from the Assessments column into the subtotal box. Then, find the total assessment figure by dividing the sum by the number of contributing factors.

RATE THE OVERALL HEALTH OF YOUR SPIRIT & SOUL ON A 1-10 SCALE: 5

SPIRIT & SOUL

CONTRIBUTING FACTORS: ASSESSMENTS	1-10	ACTIONS TO GROW
Devotions	4	✓ Find new online devo (YouVersion)
Prayer	7	✓ Consistent time; 6am; home office
Worship	7	✓ Consistent time; 6:30am; home office
Church attendance	8	✓ Weekly with family
Small group	6	✓ Block off time and recommit
Family prayer	6	✓ If out of town call in
SUBTOTAL (Sum of all contributing factor ratings)	38	TOTAL ASSESSMENT (Sub-total divided by number of contributing factors): 6.3

For example, I listed 6 contributing factors, with a subtotal of 38. I divided the subtotal (38) by 6 to find my total assessment of 6.3.

Once you have completed these exercises for each battery cell, you will have working metrics for your leadership rhythms. You will also be able to see how close your final assessment is to the initial, gut-level rating you chose. What you learn may surprise you!

You will complete two more battery cells in the same way: physical & medical and mental & emotional. Review the following examples to spark ideas for your specific contributing factors.

RATE THE OVERALL HEALTH OF YOUR SPIRIT & SOUL ON A 1–10 SCALE: 6

PHYSICAL & MEDICAL

CONTRIBUTING FACTORS

ASSESSMENTS	1-10	ACTIONS TO GROW
Fitness	5	✓ Exercise program
Body Fat %	5	✓ Nutritional plan
Cholesterol	6	✓ Eat less fat
Blood Pressure	4	✓ Reduce Stress
Sleep	6	✓ No caffeine after 1 PM
Pain	4	✓ Stretching & walking
SUBTOTAL (Sum of all contributing factor ratings)	30	TOTAL ASSESSMENT (Sub-total divided by number of contributing factors): 5

RATE THE OVERALL HEALTH OF YOUR SPIRIT & SOUL ON A 1–10 SCALE: 7

MENTAL & EMOTIONAL

CONTRIBUTING FACTORS

ASSESSMENTS	1-10	ACTIONS TO GROW
Self-talk	5	✓ Challenge thinking
Mood	5	✓ Exercise
Stress	6	✓ Unplug after 8 PM
Mental Clarity	4	✓ Regular reflection time
Personal Development	6	✓ Reading plan
Relational Health	4	✓ Invest in marriage
SUBTOTAL (Sum of all contributing factor ratings)	39	TOTAL ASSESSMENT (Sub-total divided by number of contributing factors): 6.5

RHYTHMS BATTERY CELL

Now it's your turn to consider each chamber of your personal leadership battery cells. You will assess:

- Your spirit & soul, physical & medical, mental & emotional battery cells
- The contributing factors to their health
- What action steps you must take to reach a full charge
- Your scores for each area

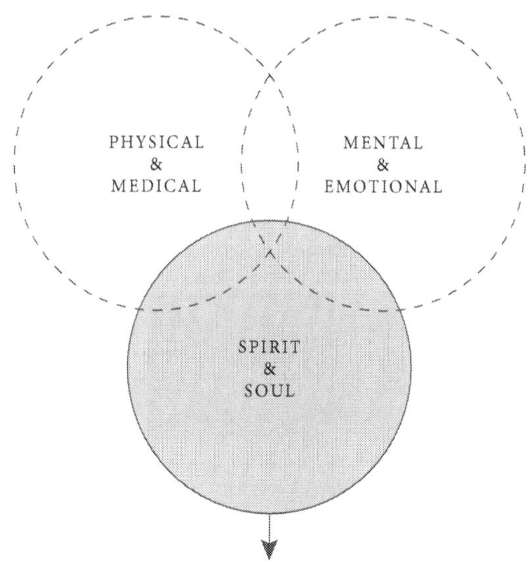

RATE THE OVERALL HEALTH OF YOUR SPIRIT & SOUL ON A 1-10 SCALE: ______

SPIRIT & SOUL

	ASSESSMENTS	1-10	ACTIONS TO GROW	
CONTRIBUTING FACTORS	• ______	☐	✓ ______	
	• ______	☐	✓ ______	
	• ______	☐	✓ ______	
	• ______	☐	✓ ______	
	• ______	☐	✓ ______	
	• ______	☐	✓ ______	
	SUBTOTAL (Sum of all contributing factor ratings)		OVERALL HEALTH (Sub-total divided by number of contributing factors)	

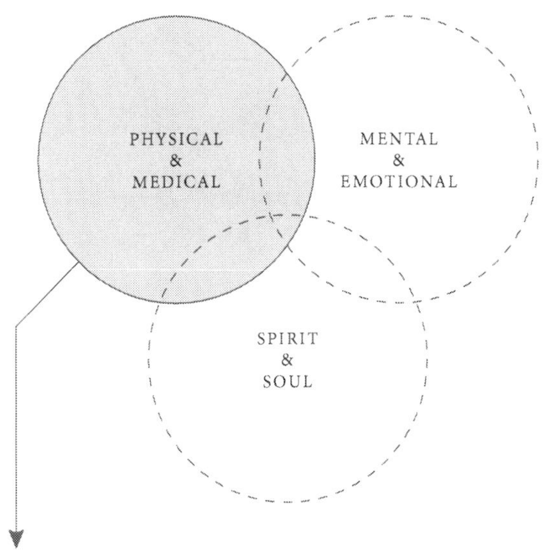

RATE YOUR OVERALL PHYSICAL & MEDICAL HEALTH ON A 1-10 SCALE: ______

PHYSICAL & MEDICAL

CONTRIBUTING FACTORS

ASSESSMENTS	1-10	ACTIONS TO GROW	
• ______	☐	✓ ______	
• ______	☐	✓ ______	
• ______	☐	✓ ______	
• ______	☐	✓ ______	
• ______	☐	✓ ______	
• ______	☐	✓ ______	
SUBTOTAL (Sum of all contributing factor ratings)		OVERALL HEALTH (Sub-total divided by number of contributing factors)	

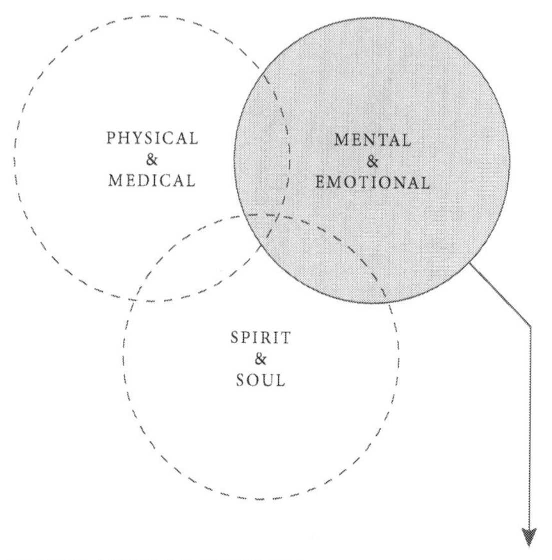

RATE YOUR OVERALL MENTAL & EMOTIONAL HEALTH ON A 1-10 SCALE: ______

MENTAL & EMOTIONAL

CONTRIBUTING FACTORS

ASSESSMENTS	1-10	ACTIONS TO GROW
* ______	☐	✓ ______
* ______	☐	✓ ______
* ______	☐	✓ ______
* ______	☐	✓ ______
* ______	☐	✓ ______
* ______	☐	✓ ______

SUBTOTAL (Sum of all contributing factor ratings)		OVERALL HEALTH (Sub-total divided by number of contributing factors)	

TAKE ACTION

Congratulations! You have just developed a winning strategy for health, wholeness, and fullness in your life.

Each chamber in your battery cell is a diagnostic tool to frequently update. High-energy leadership wins the day. So, if you find your energy levels low or your tank running dry, you can pinpoint the needed areas of renewal with accuracy.

Regardless of your current energy levels, it's never too late to live by design rather than default. My purpose is for you to reach your highest potential. If you desire to serve and steward as a leader in the Great Transfer of wealth and leadership detailed in Part One of this book, intentionally designed rhythms of renewal are the final component in the trifecta of leadership health.

ACTION ITEMS SUMMARY

AS LEADERS, WE GET charged when we move into action and when we mobilize others. In the following pages, you will find three Action Item Summary lists—one for each area you've just worked through.

Please populate each summary page with:

- The action item itself (be as clear *and* specific as possible)
- The deadline the action should be done by (date and time)
- The person responsible for execution (you may delegate an action item)

Once you have populated all of the actions, it's important to place recurring and project activities into your calendar or task management system, scheduling the action items for the day and time of completion.

As this book comes to an end, I want you to know that this final step is perhaps the most important: act on the potentially life-changing information you've just received and created. It is my objective to move you into action so you can enjoy the results of living a life of integrity and design.

This is the moment where you accelerate in your faith, seize the marriage you've always wanted, reconcile that relationship, get into the best shape of your life, build that amazing business you've always dreamed of, invest in your children, mentor others, establish that advisory board to gather the wisdom you need to grow, and so on. This is where you experience the fruit of intentional living and the peace of living a life without regret.

Finally, I offer you this challenge. Take what you have learned and teach it to at least one other individual or group. If you do, you will multiply your impact by tens-of-thousands of people over the course of your life. You will leverage yourself and impact both current *and future generations* of leaders.

May each and every one of you be inspired and equipped to maximize your potential.

To your good success!
– PHIL NICAUD

This Book of the Law shall not depart from your mouth, but you shall meditate in it day and night, that you may observe to do according to all that is written in it. For then you will make your way prosperous, and then you will have good success.
Joshua 1:8 NKJV

RELATIONSHIPS: ACTION ITEMS

Action Item	Responsible?	Deadline

All action items scheduled, delegated, or input into your task management system?

☐ Yes

RESOLUTIONS: ACTION ITEMS

Action Item	Responsible?	Deadline

All action items scheduled, delegated, or input into your task management system? ☐ Yes

RHYTHMS: ACTION ITEMS

Action Item	Responsible?	Deadline

All action items scheduled, delegated, or input into your task management system?

☐ Yes

ACKNOWLEDGEMENTS

★ ★ ★

MY WIFE

Alisa, I'm so glad your banking manager gave you permission to give me your number back in 1996! Neither one of us could have ever imagined the adventure in store for us on that fateful day! I love you with all that I am, my dear. Thank you for supporting me and our family so selflessly all of these years!

MY FAMILY

This book is a part of your heritage. My hope is that our family would be known for Sterling Character and Integrity in all matters of life, and that our world is a better place because of it!

MY MOTHERS

Bonnie (Mom) and Ann (Mom in Love), you have both been such an encouragement to me, Alisa, and our family. You two women are among the most courageous people I know. I love you both!

MY FRIENDS

Steve Robinson, though you are my pastor, you are the closest friend I have this side of Heaven. The impact that you and Jenn have had in our lives is immeasurable. Your fingerprints and footsteps are evident throughout the pages of this book and your legacy lives on as each person applies the truth of this work in their own life!

Kevin Schneider, this book would not be possible without your undying belief and investment in me and the message of *Our Secret Life*. May God richly bless you for injecting faith, life, and resources into this project!

MY MENTORS

Daniel Harkavy, your words helped restore my relationship with my father, for which I will be forever grateful. Your ongoing friendship means more to me than you will ever know!

Bob Jenks, there is no one like you, Papa Bob! I am deeply grateful for our friendship and your investment in my life. Know that your investment will multiply for generations.

MY BOARD

Mike Nicaud Sr., every time I get around you I learn something new, Uncle Mikey! I am truly grateful for you and Aunt Cindy and the wonderful example that you are to so many.

Gary Borgstede, I am so grateful for your investment and wisdom, Pastor Gary. Your faith in me and this project has given me the courage to step out and fulfill my purpose.

Brandon Schaefer, everybody needs a coach...but God blessed me with you, a leader of leaders. Truly grateful for you, Coach Brandon!

MY PASTORS

David DeGarmo, Randy Craighead, Doug Armond, and Danny Mequet, your prayers, encouragement and support over the years have shaped who I am as a father, husband, and leader. The Nicaud family is eternally grateful for your investment in our lives.

MY HEROES

General Charles Krulak – Semper Fi! Coach Tom Mullins – God bless you coach! Carl Franzella – Grazie amico mio! I admire each one of you men greatly and am so grateful for your leadership in my life.

MY GENESIS CLIENTS

Kenny Bogle, Troy Duhon, Bo Thibaut, Duane Donner, each one of you played a foundational role in my decision to start Legendary. The Nicaud family will forever be grateful to each one of you for your faith and support over the years. Every leader we serve can connect the value that they receive back to you four outstanding men! I honor and thank you all.

ABOUT THE AUTHOR

★ ★ ★

PHIL NICAUD IS THE founder and CEO of Legendary, a management consulting firm located just north of New Orleans, Louisiana. After serving in the United States Marine Corps, Phil founded multiple businesses in a variety of industries, including hospitality and real estate. Additionally, he has served as the chairman of municipal, non-governmental, and non-profit boards.

As a chief strategist at Legendary, he has coached hundreds of top-level leaders across America. His varied background allows him to speak with authority into the many different industries he coaches clients in. He leads his clients through a unique planning process that gives them a huge advantage in reaching their potential in every area of life.

Today, Phil, his wife Alisa, and their five children live in Mandeville, Louisiana. The Nicaud family is involved in their community and passionate about serving others.

Connect with Phil:

| facebook.com/philip.nicaud

OurSecretLifeBook.com

★ ★ ★

LEGENDARY WAS STARTED TO address the needs of organizational leaders who want to lead a balanced, healthy life.

All services are designed to assist founders, CEOs, and leaders, giving them the ultimate advantage of healthy life and leadership. We understand the unique pressures and stressors that leaders carry.

Legendary uses processes and tools that have been developed over twenty years to assist leaders in clarifying their desired outcomes, developing their strategies, and executing their plans with accountability...in every area of their life.

Simply put, we inspire people to lead legendary lives!

Made in the USA
Middletown, DE
28 August 2023

37481876R00104